Not Your Mama's Bible (NUMB)

A Street-Smart Self-Development Book

PASHA TAY

SKAII PUBLISHING

CONTENTS

— · —

Warning

I am not a therapist, psychologist, or any other type of mental health professional. This book is not intended to diagnose, treat, or mitigate any type of health matter. Your life is yours.

Please consult with a professional before implementing any life-altering changes. I'm not responsible for what you choose to do or how you choose to apply the information found within the book. If you are experiencing mental health concerns, please see a specialist.

INTRODUCTION

I'm going to get straight to the point: I wrote this book, but I'm not a therapist. I'm not a billionaire, motivational speaker, or celebrity. Instead, I'm an average person who's been through some shit and yet keeps his head up, smiling. I'm a singer, songwriter, software engineer, investor, and entrepreneur. I'm a good friend and a proud immigrant. I was born wealthy, but I experienced famine. Abuse and bullies plagued me. I was toxic to myself and, unfortunately, to others too.

For many years, I wasn't a cheerful person. I couldn't accept that I was gay. I was unable to defend myself against the abuse as a child and feared everything life offered. Yet, somewhere deep inside, I still had my ambitions. I wanted to be somebody. I wanted to make something of myself. My diverse life experiences, self-analysis, meticulous self-development work, and eagerness to learn from others helped me improve my quality of life.

I got rid of the mental, social, and emotional traps that held me back from loving myself and enjoying life. Now I'm a traveler, a thrill seeker, and a fortunate person. The lessons I learned throughout my life helped me re-shape my reality, which made me a happier and more emotionally mature person. The unique experiences we have can leave a huge footprint on our perceptions of life, but we can change that.

Our mindfulness and development depend on many factors: Our surroundings, environment, experiences, pain, and the people we deal with. It all affects our mindfulness. However, when our lives go to shit, we often find blame in others, which is the wrong answer. We can't blame others or be jealous of those who may have it better than us. Instead, we can look up to them as role models, use them as mentors, and learn from them. We should learn from each other, so I want to share with everyone what I've learned.

How the Book Works

This is *Not Your Mama's Bible* (NUMB). This book is distinct from your typical self-help book because it doesn't tell you what to do. It doesn't coddle you or give you false hope. This book shows you that if you want something, go out and get it yourself. This book is about separating what's worth your time and energy from what isn't—and about how to enjoy your life better. It's a book of common sense but also of hard truths, because occasionally, what we need to hear the most are the truths that are hardest to accept. However, if we want to live our best lives, we need to be honest with ourselves. We have to accept truths we don't always want to hear.

This isn't the typical self-help book that you see on store shelves. Nothing's clearly laid out for you in a cheesy or corny manner. Those books are filled with sugar-coated pleas like "wake up with a smile every morning" or "look in the mirror and say positive affirmations to yourself." While affirmations are beneficial, life is not just about rainbows and butterflies.

I'm not saying you should be a pessimist, but you need to accept that life has its hardships just as much as it has its triumphs. It's simple and complex at the same time. Sometimes, people overthink when it's unnecessary and do the opposite when they actually need to take action. However, NUMB is more practical, even though it may come across as harsher than the other self-development books you are used to.

In layman's terms, Not Your Mama's Bible is a street-smart self-development book. Many people are NUMB instead of enjoying their lives. This book is ground zero for people tired of the rat race and emotional self-torture. It's for people who are looking to live a full life—a mentally and emotionally mature life.

You can't let others stand in your way, and you need to prioritize yourself. This book is unapologetically honest and real—because that's what life is. It's a book that will make you think—to really evaluate what you want and why you want it. This book is a compilation of the lessons I've learned, and I want to share them with as many people as possible.

We often complain about or get upset over situations that are beyond our control or that don't actually matter eventually. I couldn't understand why people struggled to enjoy life as much as I did. What appeared easy and obvious to me wasn't common sense to others. So, I decided to write a book—a book of common sense, a book full of the lessons and advice I've gathered over my short time on this earth, and a summation of my life experiences and how I understand life—the golden rules I follow to keep me level-headed and content. This book is a guide, and a set of principles I live my life by that have helped me immensely.

The book is broken into 21 chapters. After the first chapter, you are free to jump around. The chapters are more independent than dependent, so you can always come back to a chapter, read before it, or skip ahead to one that piques your interest. Some chapters may refer to other stories or rules, but they should in no way affect your understanding of the material. You're welcome to treat the chapters as independent essays.

Keep in mind every situation has an edge case—a unique set of circumstances that may not adhere to the general rule, which is okay because we're all different. As I write this, my intention is not to call anyone to action. I'm not trying to say life is simply black and white or that there are only two ways to look at a situation. I'm not trying to argue that my way is the right way and that yours is wrong. Every rule has its exceptions, and you're more than welcome to call me a dumb fuck who doesn't know shit if you happen to be an edge case.

Honestly, I don't want my readers to agree with everything I say. I want the reader to think. That's the purpose of this book. It's common knowledge that everyone is different. Because of our differences, we all think differently and independently choose behaviors that suit each of us. However, by having open minds, we can acknowledge the different perspectives of others and use them to better our own lives. As long as the gears in your mind are shifting as you read, and you have a response to my point of view, then I'm satisfied.

For people who live with mental health issues, some of what I say in this book may not apply to you, and that's okay. However, seeing a specialist might be in order. While self-help and self-development books can be helpful, they are not replacements for professional help. This book is for those who want to better their lives but may feel lost or confused about where to start—for people who want more brain food. The book is for those who want to take their lives into their own hands and stop making excuses. It's for those who are willing to accept the hard truths because that's what they'll receive. You might be offended—I use profanity and form unpopular opinions—but just know that I do this with the best of intentions, and I only want what's best for you.

However, keep in mind that what works for me might not work for you. Although I tried to keep the rules open-ended and versatile, I acknowledge your circumstances might be different. Always take everything with a grain of doubt, but all I ask is that you are open-minded. If it applies to you, try it. If it doesn't, at least try to see my point of view in case it ever does in the future.

I will not tell you that NUMB will change your life overnight, but it will give you a new perspective—a more realistic one. It covers different aspects of life that we often take for granted or don't think twice about. The wrong perspective regarding these topics can hold you back from actually enjoying your life and achieving your goals.

NUMB is the book I wish I had when I was younger: A no-bullshit, street-smart self-development book. One that is closer to reality than those sugar-coated, "affirmation-focused" books. This book is for anyone who wants to make changes in their life but doesn't know how to get started.

A Note From the Author

About "Instead of Evening Prayers"

Each chapter contains a section that's titled "Instead of Evening Prayers." I am not asking or telling you not to pray. Each person must decide for themselves if communicating with a higher power or simply talking to the universe itself is worth the time and effort. However, the Instead of Evening Prayers sections are designed to be thought-provoking and give you examples to mull over in your everyday life.

1

—·—

YOU

People Don't Give a Fuck About You

People don't care about you. We're diving into the tough shit because we all need to hear it: People do not give a flying fuck. Read it again. Chew it. Swallow it. Accept it because, somewhere deep down, I'm sure you know this. I can just imagine the outrage in your mind right now. You're probably raving about those who love you and blah, blah, blah... Of course, people in this world care for you to a certain extent, but when it comes down to it, even though they love you, they will prioritize themselves, which they should.

Like it or not, people have priorities. You might be the favorite child in the family, or you may be the second favorite. The same can be true with friends, which is totally normal and totally okay. We don't have to love or even like everyone equally. I'm not saying that there's not a single soul on this planet who doesn't genuinely love or care for you. I'm sure there is, considering you likely have parents, friends, coworkers, a partner, etc. However, the percentage of platonic love in our lives is so small.

Only one thing is constant in your life, and that is yourself. Your essence, your soul, and your being come with you from birth and accompany you throughout life. Along the way, you might have company on your journey, but the only variable you can count on is yourself. In life, we often forget this and put others ahead of ourselves. We give more to people who just give us bullshit. We forget to love ourselves, yet love others immensely. When it comes to being a little bit selfish, we give ourselves the short end of the stick. We cut corners on our health or sacrifice our own happiness instead of building boundaries with others, and today, that should end.

Prioritizing ourselves over others is healthy and normal, but it can typically leave us feeling like we're being selfish. Or if we're on the receiving end, it can make us feel alone and unimportant. People want to focus on themselves, and they are too busy focusing on their own lives to really focus on yours. It's not that they don't care, it's that they have enough on their plate without having to worry about your problems too.

Even if you have good news to share, they might be jealous of your success. If it's bad news, they may not want to be surrounded by that energy.

Even those who truly care for you can only care to a certain extent. Caring for someone else is emotionally and mentally tiring. It's difficult to be responsible for another human being and constantly try to help them, especially if they don't want the help. It's natural that people would rather not have that extra weight on their shoulders if they can help it. Not to mention, emotionally intelligent and mature people always put themselves first. It's a healthy practice—and that's how it should be.

When we grow up, we leave our parents, and later in life, they leave us. It's the natural cycle of life. The same can be said for friends—people come into our lives, and eventually, they leave, or we leave them. It works the same with our kids. We fall in love, and occasionally, we fall out of love. Our partners are interchangeable. We have new work buddies every time we switch employers. We get close with friends, but we also grow apart sometimes. The only person who always stays by your side is you—no matter what, no matter where, and no matter when.

Be your best friend. You should be the love of your life. You should be your father, your mother, the protector of the realm, Santa, or the tooth fairy. If you don't love yourself, no one else will. You should be as proud as fuck that you can thrive in life even when you're alone and the world feels like a shitty place. It will eliminate any pain in a potential relationship. Grow according to your environment, and remember that whether you're single, hanging out with friends or family, married, or living with a partner, only your being will be the same throughout the scenarios.

Care for Yourself so You Can Give to Others

All this talk about self-care nowadays, and yet still, so many people forget to put themselves first. They think it's better to run on empty and be martyrs than to take care of themselves. However, it would help if you took care of yourself in order to give back. You can't radiate happiness, love, or positivity without carrying them within. Unless you are functioning in an excellent state, you can't help the outside world. You can't enjoy this life by ignoring self-care. The highest priority in your life is yourself.

Think about a plane ride for a moment. This example is trivial, but it shows, on an elementary level, the point I'm trying to make. When you get on a plane, the flight attendant goes over the rules and explains how to use the oxygen masks.

What are the rules for using the oxygen mask?

1. Put the oxygen mask on yourself before helping others.

2. Make sure the oxygen mask is snug and secure over your nose and mouth.

3. Breathe normally.

4. Once you are set, then you can help your children, partner, or other passengers.

Why do they tell you to put on the oxygen mask before helping others? The simple answer is that you can't help anyone else if you can't help yourself first. If you're struggling to breathe, you may never even be successful in helping others, and you would both struggle.

You need to be in a fit state—physically, emotionally, and mentally—in order to take care of someone else. If you don't have the proper oxygen, you will struggle to help others and end up hurting yourself more eventually. If you're not taking care of yourself, you cannot help others. You can't pour from an empty cup because you need liquid in that cup to pour from.

Consider this example: You're on a boat with your favorite people, and it starts sinking. You're all in danger. Unless you're able to save yourself, you won't be able to save anyone else. As soon as you're saved, you can come up with a plan to save others, but if you're not, then you will drown along with everyone else.

Side note: This is also a good time to point out our priorities when it comes to saving people. Who would you save first, second, and third? Do you see how we have priorities in our minds? You still love all of them, that's for sure, but we have priorities, and you should be first.

Life Is a Stage, and You're the Actor, Director, and Screenwriter

Take a moment to imagine that you're an actor in a play. The director tells you what to do, what to say, and how to behave. You don't argue with the director; you simply do as you're told. Once the play is over, you move on to another play with another director for a unique part. You play that role, and this little pattern continues throughout your life—a never-ending cycle.

Now, imagine that life is one big play. It's an enormous stage with a never-ending supply of directors. These directors can be your parents, teachers, siblings, or even spouses. They assign you roles and tell you how to behave. You obediently follow their directions because that's what excellent actors do.

However, many miss a crucial aspect of their lives—only one rightful and qualified director of your life exists—you. Life is designed that way. If that's not the case, something went wrong at some point. Maybe you stepped out as a director or believed you were a terrible director and refused to take action, so somebody else took your place. Now they decide for you.

If that's the case, take the ownership back. You get to decide who you are, what you do, and how you behave. You get to create yourself and tell people who you are. When you decide, you can change the characters as many times as you want.

Nobody knows you as well as you do. Nobody knows who you are, and no one should ever define you. Tell people who you are and create yourself. You should be confident and let no one put you down. You should save yourself before others, because if you're not okay, then how can you expect to save anyone else? After all, your most important priority is always yourself.

Forget everything people have told you about yourself. They know nothing. Most of them don't even know who they are themselves. People fear their dreams and are petrified of failure or terrified of success—all around being fearful of everything. The only aspect of life that puts them at ease is the assurance that everyone is just like them—scared. So, to comfort themselves, they put others down and spread misery. There shouldn't be any authority in your life over your decisions, dreams, or actions. You tell them who you are or, better yet, show them. Life is your stage.

The center of the universe is you. The most important person in your life is you. It's your movie, stage, theater, or costume. You get to play all the parts. By following this nugget of information, I realized I have no obligation to be the person I was a year ago, a month ago, a week ago, or even an hour ago. I can change myself and my reality with the snap of my fingers.

I don't owe anybody shit. If I feel like an asshole, then that's what I am today. I own it if I feel like a bad bitch. I can be as sweet as molasses if I feel like the most loving person in the world. If I decide in the morning that I'm going to have a great day today, then nobody can ruin it unless I let them. If I decide to turn into a fucking astronaut, believe me, regardless of the obstacles, I will become one. No one has power over my emotions, my personality, my decisions, or my future. I'm in charge. The power is mine.

Science 101

Every living being dies, which is why I am surprised that so many people are afraid. We all meet the same fate, so what the fuck are you afraid of? Who the fuck are you trying to impress? Who the fuck are you ashamed of, and who the fuck are you living for? Only one correct answer exists to these questions: You. Don't be stupid—life goes by faster than the memory on your iPhone. Unless you're lucky and become some Mozart-type genius, there will be a maximum of two generations who will remember you. You don't need anyone's approval. You should give zero fucks whether someone approves of you or not. If they disapprove, that's their problem, not yours.

A few years ago, I learned this the hard way. I came out to a friend of mine about my sexual orientation. I was becoming more comfortable with who I am: I'm gay and proud. However, he wasn't as accepting. He said that it was difficult for him to accept my sexual orientation, but that he'd "try."

He'd try his best to "be okay" with me being gay—as if it were an enormous favor, and he should receive the Nobel Peace Prize for his generosity. Well, what could I tell him? I told him to go fuck himself. Being my friend is a damn privilege, not the other way around. Who was doing who a favor?—that was the rhetorical question, but a simple rule. If someone is not okay with who you are, they can get lost. We don't need those people.

Nobody owes you shit, and you don't owe anybody shit either. Never feel obligated to do anything for anyone—and that includes your parents. It doesn't matter who's in front of you. If you have no urge or desire to perform an action, don't even bother. Saying no is an important, but tough lesson to implement. Prioritizing yourself is critical to your success and happiness. I'm not saying you should be a jerk and ignore everybody. You don't have to be that cocky asshole. I'm saying that you shouldn't step over yourself and do something your heart is not willing to do. Listen to yourself.

Throughout my years on this earth, I've witnessed toxic parents acting manipulatively toward their kids. They say common phrases like, "I brought you into this world," "I feed you and care for you," "I gave you the roof over your head," and so on and so forth. One day I had the, as they call it, "audacity" to share my opinions with my dear friend's mother. I merely mentioned that their kids didn't appear out of thin air, unannounced. The parents had children. The mother created the obligation for herself. She had children for herself because that's what she wanted, so it shouldn't be presented as a favor to the child.

If you are on the other end of the spectrum and wish to have a child who will care for you, show them by example. Love that child instead of manipulating them. You will always harvest whatever you have planted. You can't expect an apple from an orange tree. Treat your children well, and they will help you when they can, but don't expect help, empathy, or support. Remember, nobody owes you shit. So, don't get offended when people ignore you and don't treat you like the king of the universe. That's your job, not theirs.

Kindness Is an Unnecessary Transaction—But a Delightful One

Always think about people's kindness as a courtesy, as a delightful bonus—but just that, an extra. If someone shows they care, never take it for granted. Take it as a life bonus point. Take it as a blessing and give thanks to that person. It doesn't matter how. Always recognize that kindness and show your gratitude.

You can do it through an action, a warm thank you, or a compliment. It doesn't matter, but do your best to appreciate what people are giving to you. They don't have to do it, but kindness is like a currency, and the sooner you understand that life is essentially a global transactional system, the sooner you will start enjoying the outcomes of every transaction you are exposed to.

The most recent "transaction" that popped into my head actually happened yesterday when I was checking into a hotel. I was tired and felt like shit. I asked the front desk lady if there would be breakfast available and if it was included in the price. She said it's not included, and that the breakfast buffet costs $30 per person. Then, she just pulled a breakfast voucher for me for no official reason, only to make my stay more pleasant. She didn't have to do it. She wasn't the manager or owner of the property. She did it because she wanted to be nice and warm-hearted.

I felt like being nice too, so I returned the transaction. I cracked a few jokes just to make her laugh—to brighten up her day some. It was a successful transaction, in my opinion. When I'm in a good mood and I feel like being nice, I randomly give to people just like she did to me, and people respond the same way—by returning the transaction.

Nobody owes you shit. You're not required to give to others, and they're not required to give to you. It's a harsh reality to accept. We want others to give to us because we feel that we're good people and deserve it. However, nobody is in our debt. We're all just individuals trying to make our way in the world.

To offset this, you can make this better for yourself by randomly giving to others. Giving to others feels good, and it's a great way to make someone's day. Plus, you never know when you'll need someone to lend a hand. When you give to others with a pure heart and good intentions, you plant a seed of positivity and love, which the world could use more of. Expect nothing in return, though, because nobody owes you anything.

Instead of Evening Prayers

1. Ask yourself who you want to be. What is your ideal situation or environment? Picture that persona in your head in vivid detail. Describe that character to yourself—how does this person look, speak, and act? If you wish, name

the character. When the character is ready, it's time to shine. Open the stage curtains and play that character.

2. Practice regular gratitude when people are kind to you. Even if the gesture is insignificant. Genuinely convey your appreciation. You can say, "thank you," give a compliment, tell a joke, provide some assistance—whatever you feel like giving back. Keep those transactions rolling, and watch as they come back to you.

3. Schedule a date with yourself. You can treat yourself to a delicious meal, or draw a fine-ass bath with candles, bath bombs, and all that boujie crap. Take a vacation or just a good book. You know yourself best, so pick something you'll enjoy. Make sure to always treat yourself first and well. Work yourself into your routine.

2

Not So Secret Sauce

Confidence.

What is it? A personality trait? A skill? An accident of birth?

For our purposes, confidence is best described as a state of mind. It's the result of having faith in yourself and your ability to meet challenges. It's feeling sure of your own value and capabilities, which is an essential ingredient of achieving success.

Confidence Smells Good, Looks Good, and Feels Good

Have you noticed two people can wear the same outfit, but one will look stunning and the other will look awkward? How is that possible? Well, you know it has nothing to do with biological features, right? It's all about confidence. It's all about how you carry yourself.

Confidence is the key. It's not a secret, but people still disregard this important aspect of self-development. Before putting on that gorgeous attire of yours, make sure you are wearing confidence underneath.

Confidence is the one quality that you can fake until you make it, and it is worth faking because it will change your life. It will make you feel better about yourself, and it will also make other people see you in a different light. When you walk into a room with your head held high and a smile on your face, people notice. They see you as someone who is comfortable in their own skin and someone who is worth talking to.

Think about it: Would you be more likely to achieve your goals if you believed in yourself or doubted yourself? The answer is obvious. The same is true of other people. We're more likely to trust and follow those who seem confident than those who seem unsure of themselves. Hence, confidence is a crucial quality in leaders.

It's attractive and contagious. Confidence is not about being liked. Confidence is about giving zero fucks if people like you or not. Being the one people want to like is about confidence. Confidence starts with changing the way you think about yourself. Once you see yourself in a positive light, that's when the magic happens.

Luckily, you can develop confidence. It's not a fixed quality like the color of your eyes or the shape of your nose. It's a muscle that you can strengthen with use. The more you use it, the stronger it will become.

Confidence Comes From Results

People are rarely born confident. This quality is developed over time. The more you achieve, the more confident you become. Why? Because results give you proof that you can do it. They give you evidence that you're competent. When you can look back and see all the tasks you've accomplished, it's easier to believe in yourself and your abilities.

You develop confidence by taking risks and putting yourself out there, even if you're not sure you'll succeed. Confidence is about stepping outside of your comfort zone and learning from your mistakes. Every time you step outside your comfort zone, you're building your confidence. Confidence is the key to success. Confidence prompts you to take risks and pursue your dreams. It's something everyone can cultivate. Strengthen your confidence muscle and see what you can achieve.

Of course, confidence doesn't just come from enormous accomplishments. You can build confidence through small wins. Every time you accomplish a goal, no matter how big or small, it's an opportunity to build your confidence. The more confident you become, the more likely you are to take risks and pursue your dreams. Confidence is a critical ingredient in success.

Confidence is a quality we have to work on. It doesn't come naturally to everyone. We have to cultivate confidence. Confidence can be built, but it can also be destroyed. Concentrate on who you want to be—all day, every day—and not on how you are afraid to appear. This is one of the few exceptions where you should actually fake it until you make it.

Not everybody has confidence in themselves. Insecurity might have eaten them up, or they may simply never have learned how to be confident. Sometimes it's just the way we are. Sometimes it's the consequence of abuse, mistreatment, or bullying. Whatever happened to you, drop that heavy bag immediately and repaint yourself. You should never give up on confidence. It's the most important quality you need in order to succeed.

By carrying those tragedies that cracked or destroyed your confidence, you will appear as a victim—as a weak person. People can sense those vibes, and some will follow the threat. On a subconscious level, people read your personality print as a manual to you, and people can read others very well. If you don't believe in yourself, why should they? They read the instructions and then apply them. If they see changes in the manual, they make adjustments. You are free to change or adjust a manual for yourself as often and as much as you wish. Use whatever tools come your way. Reshape yourself. Grow confidence.

The solution is not to act like someone else. Be the best version of yourself. It might sound cliché, but it's true. The problem with low confidence is that it's a self-fulfilling prophecy. When you don't believe in yourself, you're less likely to take risks or pursue your dreams. As a result, you accomplish little, and your lack of confidence becomes justified. The only way to break this cycle is to take action and start building your confidence.

Our human nature is attracted to confidence, and your life will be easier if you're confident. If you're not confident, you're going to have to work a lot harder to get what you want. Success attracts confident people. When you're confident, people are more likely to listen to, trust, and follow you.

So, wear your low-key, favorite, yet ugly, and over-sized hoodie that you inherited from your brother with pride, and people will see the Ariana Grande style ooze from you. If you wear it like it's an itchy prison, then people will think you're a broke-ass bitch. However, don't let confidence fool you. Don't let your confidence give you a colossal head and turn you into a snob.

Even though we want to look like we know every fuck-ing thing, we need to keep our ears and eyes open and learn. Knowledge is power. You may think you know all the facts on a certain topic, but there is always something to learn—and that's also part of building confidence. So, don't forget: Stay humble and keep learning.

Truth Is Subjective

One of the biggest obstacles to confidence is the belief that there's only one right way to do a task or achieve a goal—that there's only one truth with a capital "T." This can lead to many problems because it means that we're constantly comparing ourselves to an im-possible ideal—striving for the nonexistent. We think we should be thinner, smarter, more successful, or whatever, and when we're not, we feel like failures.

Truth doesn't have a single absolute. Truth is subjective. What's true for one person may not be true for another.

We struggle to accept this concept because we've learned that truth is objective, i.e., 2 + 2 = 4, and that's just the way it is. Depending on the context, what initially seems true can be a figment of our imaginations—like a mirage. Don't get hung up on what's *supposed* to be true.

When you view the truth from an open-minded perspective, it opens up a variety of possibilities. You can create your own reality, rather than being a victim of circumstance. You create the truth. If you make other people believe in something, it becomes their truth. You have the power to make yourself whole, create your own truth, and bring it to the masses.

People view us through a lens, just like a camera. The lens is shaped by what you offer them. Don't give them a blurry mess. Craft the lens carefully. Make as many lenses as you need. Life is about making mistakes and learning from them. The more you tackle challenges, the more confident you'll become. Create a lens for different people, unique situations, and distinct atmospheres. That lens is up to you, and you decide how people view you.

Ask and You Shall Receive

Part of having confidence is believing that you deserve good things. It sounds simple, but many of us go through life feeling like we don't deserve success or happiness. We think we're not good enough, smart enough, or talented enough. As a result, we don't even try.

Like Selena Gomez asked, "Who said that?" Who said you don't deserve positivity, prosperity, and wealth? We all deserve a life full of positivity. We just have to believe it and ask for it. If you don't ask, you'll never get what you want.

Yes, while we discussed that no one owes you anything, we're not talking about expecting people to give you what you haven't earned. Asking for what you deserve—like respect, love, and appreciation—is what I'm talking about. We need to stop thinking that we don't deserve these perks, because we all deserve to be loved and respected. Just ask for them.

Do you want that promotion? Ask for it. Do you want more responsibility at work? Ask for it. Do you want to be in a relationship? Ask for it. Do you not like the coffee you ordered? Ask for a new one. The bottom line is that if you don't ask, you definitely won't get what you want. If you do ask, the worst that can happen is that the person will say, "No," but even that can be a learning opportunity. If you don't get what you want, ask yourself why. What could you have done differently? How can you improve your chances next time? Some people are afraid to ask for what they want because they don't want to be seen as pushy, demanding, or selfish. You'll never get ahead in life if you don't at least try to ask.

To increase your chances of success, you need your confidence, which is why I reinforced the importance of this quality. You need to believe in yourself and your abilities. Saying no to confident people is tough because they ooze self-assurance. They give off the impression that they will not take "no" for an answer. They're going to get what they want, one way or another. When you're confident, people are more likely to say, "Yes" to you. Of course, you have to be reasonable, and you should always consider the context. However, the main point is to use confidence with every task you take on.

Confidence is a spice you use to make your life a bomb meal. It allows you to take risks, face adversities, and achieve your goals. It's the key to success.

Instead of Evening Prayers

1. Pause here for just a moment to evaluate your confidence. Are you confident? If not, list the reasons that contribute to your lack of self-belief. Write them down and reevaluate each reason. Eliminate each one by coming up with ways you can counteract the belief. Little goals, actions, and successes build enormous confidence. It is a process. There's no magical pill. It's a positive side effect of eliminating things you are just not good at. Simple. No one is good at everything.

2. While working on building that inner confidence, you can use some tricks to confuse people. Instead of them reading your personality manual, redirect them to the banner that reads, *Confidence is in the works. The Grand Opening is coming soon.* This means applying tricks that will make you appear more confident. Fake it by fixing your posture (stand tall), voice (lower the pitch, and speak clearly, loudly, and slowly), eyes (keep eye contact), and body language (no

crossing your arms and be relaxed). Do some research on how to appear more confident. I will not go into detail here. Otherwise, this book would be a two-for-one.

3. Start developing a habit of being confident. I am pretty sure there are plenty of situations where you wanted to take action but were reluctant. From now on, do not allow yourself to hide. Start speaking up and standing up for yourself. Create situations where confidence is involved. For example, start a conversation with a random stranger at a coffee shop, bar, café, or gas station. Be as creative as you want. Just start doing it—expose yourself to it.

3

— • —

CRY ME A RIVER

We've all been there before. You're mindlessly scrolling through social media when you see it: A post from that one person who just can't seem to stop complaining about their mishaps. You know the type—they're unhappy with their job, significant other, or life in general, but do little to fix it. Even when they experience positivity, they complain about it. Or maybe you're that person.

Life is hard. Life is unfair. Both statements are accurate. Some people are more fortunate than we are, while others aren't. That will always be the case. Comparing ourselves to others and justifying our complaints is human nature—but guess what? You can either cry in every corner or you can try to do your best to enjoy life. Complaining doesn't change our circumstances. In fact, it only makes a situation worse because negativity breeds more negativity.

When we complain, we focus on the terrible aspects of our lives and cannot see the good that surrounds us. So, what can we do instead? When facing a difficult situation, try to find a silver lining. Maybe that difficult situation is just what we need to grow and become the people we want to be. Maybe it's an opportunity to help someone else who is experiencing the same challenges.

The next time you complain, remember this: Life is hard. Life is unfair, but it's also beautiful. Don't let the negative outweigh the positive. Life is all about balance, so try to find joy or a benefit from every situation and enjoy the life you're living. If you're negative or dramatic, change your perspective because life is too short to complain all the time. Find joy in the tiny transactions that life hands you and be grateful for what you have. Shit happens—learn from it.

Don't Be a Whiner

You probably know a person or two who seem to always struggle, right? This is the person who has an evident problem in every area of their life, and they've been climbing the mountain for years. Every time you see them, they reveal their latest tragedy. Maybe you ask them how they're doing, and they go on this long, depressing rant about how terrible everything is.

This person is a whiner, and we all know that whiners are annoying as fuck. What emotion do you experience when you think about those people? Do you like being around people like that? I know I don't. I avoid them because people who complain all the time about every fucking thing are as toxic as shit. Deep down, they don't want or need any of our help. If you offer them advice, they'll argue and point out all the flaws. They complain just to hear themselves talk and to make other people feel uncomfortable.

Complaining is part of their routine—it's a habit. They see you as a public toilet where they can shit whenever they feel like it. Have you ever heard of the term "emotional vampire?" That's a whiner. They feed off your emotional responses to their complaints. Sometimes they are just so fucking bored with their miserable lives and have nothing else to do. Their hobby is to shit around. If you have people like that in your life, run. Isolate yourself from them. Remove them from your life as soon as possible. Treat them as cancerous cells that poison your environment.

That negativity is unnecessary in your life. Just say no. Let them know you will not tolerate their shitty attitude and that they need to take their crap some-where else. Do what you can to protect your emotion-al well-being. The best way to deal with this type of person is to just walk away. Don't even engage with them. They're not worth your time or energy. Just politely excuse yourself and walk away. If you have to, just say, "I'm sorry, I don't want to talk about that," and walk away. It's so stupidly simple, and yet people complicate it. You don't have to tolerate their crap. You don't have to be friends with them. You don't even have to be nice to them. Just walk away and don't look back.

Last year, my friend Camilla had to be the head of the complaint department. Every time she saw me, she shared every tiny problem in her life. She wasn't just talking about normal, everyday problems—I'm refer-ring to the same problem she's had for years and has done nothing about. She talked incessantly about is-sues with her family, friends, job, love life, weight, and even her cat-like, who the fuck complains to people about their cat? She always had a challenge to face, even though the cat was the least of her problems.

I tried my best to be a good friend and listen to her, but after a while, I just couldn't take it anymore. One day, we sat down, and I explained that I didn't want to hear her whine. She couldn't expect me to fix her life.

I understood she was going through a tough time, but I couldn't bear to be her sounding board forever. She needed to look for solutions instead of wallowing in her problems.

For the next few months, she took it well, and I heard little complaining from her. Then, out of the blue, she started up again with the same old bullshit stories. This time, she was worse. She would call me to go on and on about how much her life sucked and how everyone was out to get her. Silly me tried to help her again.

As she complained about her weight, I offered her nutrition advice and invited her to the gym with me, which she dismissed. She ignored the job postings and resume tips I sent as she complained. When she whined about her love life, I set her up on blind dates, which she blew off. I even offered to help her move when she complained about her living situation, but she refused.

I did what I could to help her, but she wasn't interested in taking any responsibility for her own life. She wanted me to be a personal cheerleader, but I couldn't do that anymore. So, I walked away. Other people might actually need me and appreciate my help, so that's where I focused my energy instead of on some whining-ass bitch.

These people are everywhere, and if you're not careful, you'll become one yourself. The trap of complaining and negativity is a slippery slope; we all have the potential to be whiners. Only some of us have learned how to control it and focus on the positive, while others have let it run their lives. I'm not saying that you should never talk about your problems or be negative. We all have our down days, but be mindful of how often you're complaining and focus on more positives instead.

I'm not perfect, and I have definitely complained from time to time—about the weather, my job, and everything in between. There is, however, a balance to be struck, and I think it's important to see the good in every situation rather than just dwell on the negative.

Don't be a whiner—don't be one of those people. Focus on the positive and make the best of every situation. It's not always easy, but it's worth it. Do not complain to others about every single thing. It will only make them not want to be around you. Try to be more positive, even if your life is not going the way you want it to. Whining only makes the experience worse.

Everyone has their own routine problems to deal with. Before sharing something with others, ask yourself: What is the reason behind the complaint? Do you need advice? If so, then share. Do you need or want help? Good. Then share. Do you just want to let off some steam and talk to someone? Great, then speak up, but know your limits and know who you are sharing with. Do you think it's entertaining for someone with whom you want to share it? Good—spill that tea. You get the point—share for a reason, not to spread the pain. Never share just to complain or cry, and don't overdo it. Always keep in mind—people should be excited about chatting with you. If you are draining them, you are a vampire.

At the same time, however, don't let your emotions build up inside of you to the point where they explode. Find a healthy balance between talking about your problems and keeping them to yourself. Don't lock yourself up and stop sharing with your people. We all need an annual Cry Day. Otherwise, we will lose our shit. Express your emotions and share when you need to. Just don't make it your default personality trait or a routine. Don't be the crying baby. Always decide between "The world is happening to you" or "The world is happening for you." I chose the second.

Solve Your Problems ASAP

Complaining might make you feel better momentarily, but the best thing you can do for yourself when you have a problem is to take action to solve it. If you're unhappy with your job, look for a new one. If you're unhappy with your significant other, talk to them about it. Don't sit on your ass and complain because that won't improve your situation. If an answer doesn't exist, learn to accept it and move on.

Most aspects of life are out of our control, like the weather or traffic. While venting might ease stress initially, what will make you feel better throughout the day and the rest of the week is to find the good that can come from it. Maybe now you have an excuse to stay in and watch a movie or take a nap. Or perhaps being stuck in traffic gives you the opportunity to call a friend you haven't spoken to in a long time. Use that time to improve your mood—not become more salty.

Learn from the experience, appreciate that it's not worse than it could be, be grateful for what you have, and move the fuck on.

The Colors of Sadness Are the Same for Everyone

Remember when I said some people are more or less fortunate than we are? Well, it's true. Some people have bigger problems than you do. Some people have smaller problems, but it's all about perspective. The root of the problem isn't the real concern. Suffering is an experience we can all relate to. From your perspective, life may seem like one big problem, but there's always someone who has it worse than you. If complaining isn't accompanied by an action, it solves nothing. Instead of complaining, be thankful for what you have. Our actions are contagious. So, don't be the one who spreads complaints. You can choose not to complain. No one is forcing you to complain. You're choosing to focus on the negative.

Of course, you might have a tight-knit circle of friends or family members who love to complain along with you. However, even they would probably appreciate more positivity from you. They might listen to your drama, but they will most likely get tired of it after a while. They have their own problems and can't solve all of yours. If you share them with your friends, don't overdo it. Follow the five-minute rule.

Vent for five minutes to release the weight from your chest, but not to seek answers. Your friends likely won't have them, but if you keep your complaints to a minimum, they'll be more likely to listen. You're the only one responsible for your attitude and problems. Be the person who brightens up the room with your positive attitude. Sadness doesn't discriminate. It doesn't matter who you are or what you have; everyone experiences sadness at some point in their lives. You don't have to wallow in it and complain about it.

When someone shares with you something that seems insignificant to you, it may be a big deal for them. We all have our own problems, and we deal with them differently. Someone else's issues might not seem as big as yours, but that doesn't mean they're invalid. Consider that, and be sympathetic instead of dismissive toward a friendly face. Don't depreciate someone's pain because you cannot relate to it. If they're searching for help, and you can give it, then do so. Provide them with a solution, advice, empathy, or comfort. If not, just be there to listen and offer emotional support. If you want to understand, ask questions. But learn to tell the difference between people who really want and need your help and whiny bitches.

Instead of Evening Prayers

1. Turn your awareness to the minor pleasures in life and practice gratitude. Here's a fun practice for you: A positive experience jar. At the end of each week, take a piece of colored paper and scribble every nice or exciting occurrence you've experienced. Fold it up and drop it in the jar. Near the end of the year, like Christmas or New Year's Eve, grab the jar and review the year. Randomly pull out each note, read it, and re-experience what you wrote. Just enjoy every outstanding memory and let it flow through you.

2. Find a reason to smile at least once every single day. The more, the better. Are birds chirping outside your window? Pause for a second to enjoy it and smile. Drinking morning coffee? Inhale the aroma and smile. Is there a cute couple seated next to you? Feel happy for them and smile. If someone compliments you, appreciate it. Feel good about yourself. We have thousands of reasons to smile per day. Learn to spot the

reasons and make it a habit to, you guessed it, smile.

3. Evaluate the people you are interacting with daily. Are there any whining bitches who are constantly dumping their shit on you? Deal with them once and for all. Either reevaluate your boundaries or cut them off completely. Detox from any emotional poison. You don't need that shit.

4

— · —

BORDER CONTROL

You know that feeling when someone tries to hug you, and you're just kind of standing there like a stiff board? Or when someone asks you a question, and you give them an empty stare because your mind goes totally blank?

Yeah, that's what it feels like when you have no boundaries. A boundary is like a line that you draw in the sand—a limit that you set for yourself in order to protect your energy, time, space, and sanity. Without boundaries, we are like doormats that people can just wipe their feet on. We end up feeling used, abused, and taken advantage of.

Without boundaries, we can't say, "no" when we need to, and we can't stick up for ourselves when someone crosses the line. People can allow themselves to cross lines they shouldn't. They can get too personal. They can hurt you, and you can't really blame them for it because they were operating within the perimeters that you created.

Setting boundaries was something that I struggled with for a long time. I was a people pleaser, and I didn't want to rock the boat. However, I learned the hard way that not setting boundaries leads to people taking advantage of you. I allowed myself to be treated poorly because I was afraid of speaking up. I allowed people to walk all over me, and I allowed myself to be taken advantage of.

Apply a Lock and Control the Key

Locks are on the front door of your house, car, phone, and even computer for a reason: To keep people from just walking in and taking your shit. The same should apply to your personality. You should apply a lock on your personality. You can't let anyone come in and do whatever the fuck they want. Someone being "nice" doesn't mean they get a free pass into your life. In order to have thriving relationships, both personal and professional, it is essential that you set boundaries.

You should have rules and regulations set in place for the people in your life. Just like a business has rules and regulations set in place for its employees, you need to create them for the people in your life. The people who are allowed in should be there because they respect your boundaries. If someone can't respect your rules, then they don't need to be in your life.

The rules can either be different or the same for each person. We can't always agree with everyone. It all depends on you and what you're comfortable with. No right or wrong answer applies to boundaries, as long as you are true to yourself. It's your chamber. You get to choose who comes in and who doesn't. You protect it as you wish.

The radius at which you create your fence is also up to you. It can be as small or as large as you want it to be. Just remember, the larger the fence, the more people you can let in. The smaller the fence, the more intimate the people become, and the more people you tell to fuck off. Create what you're looking for and what you're comfortable with. It can be different depending on the person, situation, or even the day. Some relationships require more intimacy than others. The key is to be mindful of your personal space and energy. Then act accordingly. The boundaries have to be there for a reason, and that reason is always *you*.

There will be times when people will test your boundaries. They will try to see how much they can get away with before you put your foot down. Testing boundaries is an annoying but normal habit, and it's to be expected. Just remember, you are in charge of your life and decide who can enter. Don't let anyone take advantage of you or make you feel like you owe them shit. You are not obligated to explain yourself to anyone. Your boundaries are your boundaries, and that's all there is to it.

If someone can't respect your fucking simple, yet crucial boundaries, then get rid of them—throw them out. Don't be a garbage collector—something we'll visit in Chapter 7.

It's that simple.

Set Boundaries Through Your Tones and Radiation

Your tone and the way you carry yourself will also help to set boundaries. Your verbal and nonverbal communication should be in alignment with what you're trying to channel. If you're trying to keep people at a distance, then your tone and body language should reflect that. If you're trying to be more open and inviting, then your tone and body language should convey that.

The same goes for your personal space. If you're trying to keep people at a fucking distance, then you'll want to make sure you have plenty of personal space. If you're comfortable with people being closer to you, then you'll want to make sure your personal space reflects that.

Your energy also plays a role in setting boundaries. If you're feeling overwhelmed or drained, then your energy will reflect that. If you're feeling happy and healthy, that translates to your energy too. Pay attention to your energy and how it's affecting your interactions with others. If you're feeling off, then it's probably best to take some time for yourself to recharge.

For example, if you allow some disrespectful jokes or comments just once, you're setting the boundaries with that person by doing so and teaching people it's okay for them to operate within that space. It also goes both ways. If you allow yourself to say certain phrases or sit within a specific space, then you are creating boundaries for that person to follow. You showed the person what was acceptable by your standards.

People will use the feedback you give them to gauge how far they can push. The best way to set boundaries is by example. The distance, tone, and environment are created by you. You operate within that space with the other person. It is your responsibility to make sure that space is comfortable for you. No one can do that for you.

In most cases, it will stay that way until one of you tries to change it. There will be a push and pull as you both try to establish your own boundaries. Remember, you have the right to say, "no," and to set your own boundaries. You don't have to stay NUMB and give in to people who are used to getting what they want. In fact, it's often best to stand your ground and be firm about what you will and won't tolerate. If they are successful in pushing your boundaries, meaning that you don't show noticeable effects of their attempts, then they will continue to do so until you introduce fresh changes.

Sometimes people misinterpret or ignore the boundaries. In that case, you must speak up! You can't let people walk all over you or take advantage of you. That's not fair to you, and it's not healthy for them either. If you don't set boundaries, then people will continue to take advantage of you, and that's not a healthy way to live.

My dear friend Tanisha is a perfect example of someone who has mastered the art of setting boundaries. She is clear, concise, and firm about what she will and won't tolerate. She's a sweet woman, but she knows what she wants, and she's not afraid to stand up for herself. I admire her for that.

You see, a few months ago, she started dating a new guy. He was charming, funny, and good-looking. Tanisha was smitten. However, one morning, they were goofing around, and her boyfriend flipped her the bird. To him, it was funny—an innocent joke. To her, it was disrespectful and immature.

Tanisha didn't hesitate to speak up. She didn't appreciate being disrespected, and it wasn't funny to her. Tanisha told him, "Please never do that again." She established her boundaries in the situation. It didn't matter that to her boyfriend, it wasn't a big deal because, for Tanisha, it wasn't acceptable. The situation never occurred again. This example may be simple and innocent, but it goes to show you how powerful setting boundaries can be. It's critical to communicate and cut the tree down before it becomes an Amazon forest.

Instead of Evening Prayers

1. Are there any people you are not happy with or with whom you wish to change the boundaries? To eliminate undesirable behavior, you must make changes. List the changes you want to make in the relationship. Talk to that person and start working on the new boundary line with them pronto.

5

_—·—_

ESSENTIAL SKILLS

In life, we need certain skills to make it to the top. In my opinion, among these skills, psychology and sales are two of the most important ones. Why is that? Simply put, these two qualities go hand in hand. In order to be a successful salesperson, you need to understand psychology. Understanding the whys and hows of people and their actions, along with applying sales tricks, can land you anything you want in life.

If you want to be successful in anything you do, whether it's your career, your relationships, or your personal life, you need to understand and use psychology through sales techniques.

The Secret Essential Skills of Any Goal

Psychology is the study of the human mind. It helps us understand why people think and behave the way they do. You can't get through life without encountering psychology. Psychology is everywhere—from the way you talk to your friends to the way you negotiate with your boss. If you want to be successful, you need to understand psychology. We interact with people from the day we are born until the day we die. By nature, we are social creatures, and the art of reading and understanding people is crucial.

If we could read people, understand them better, see their needs, and comprehend their points of view, it would be easier to interact with them. It would eliminate lots of stress, misunderstandings, unnecessary arguments, attitudes, confusion, and pain. Seeing people for their uniqueness and quirks is one of the most valuable skills you can possess. The benefits are 360, meaning that this skill will improve all areas of your life. By seeing the world from different perspectives, you can ensure that people will also feel appreciated, valued, and respected. You can either build a better relationship or you can avoid hazardous human interactions. Understanding psychology is like holding a crystal ball in your hands and getting a glimpse into your future with a person.

Sales, on the other hand, is the art of persuasion. In order to be successful in any field, you need to sell. Whether you're selling a product, an idea, or yourself, the ability to sell is essential.

When you think about it, life is one big sales pitch. You're always selling something, whether it's an idea to your boss, a product to a customer, or yourself to a potential date. We are selling our desires to loved ones, school projects to teachers, candidacies to colleges, skills to employers, business ideas to investors, dream vacations to our partners, or TV shows we love and books we enjoy. We are constantly selling things. Our life is a huge, never-ending market. The better your sales skills, the better results you get in every aspect of life. Plus, you would accomplish your goals more quickly and with less stress.

Some people are naturally born with empowering sales abilities. They can sell water to fish or a car to a dealership. For the rest of us, persuasion is something we need to learn and practice. Like any skill, it takes time to master, but if you can master the art of selling, you will be successful in every area of your life.

My friend Kareem has always worked in the service industry. He had never had a corporate position or owned a business, but he wanted to try a corporate career. He applied for the lowest entry-level positions in many companies but wasn't receiving any calls. As we sat down to discuss his job search strategy, he told me his end goal was to work in HR. He loved working with people, but since he never had office or HR experience, he wasn't qualified.

He became discouraged and thought about giving up on his dream. "Who am I kidding? I should just go back to a restaurant—it's what I'm good at. I mean, I have tremendous experience, and besides, I'm too old to change careers," he told me quietly.

This was an opportunity to sell Kareem to himself. I asked him, "Who made your resume?"

"I did, of course."

"Well, that's an HR experience. How well do you work with different people?"

"I get along well with others. I worked as a server and a bartender for a long time," he told me. "I've dealt with thousands of people throughout my career."

"Isn't that a major qualification for HR? To be a people-person? What about your technology skills? Would you say you're tech-savvy?" I asked.

"I'm very good with tech. I was the one who taught new employees how to use the POS system at the restaurant."

"So, you can easily pick up new technology? I'm assuming you can learn the tech systems of an HR department?"

"Yes, absolutely," he replied with a little more enthusiasm.

"Have you ever helped with interviewing and onboarding?"

"Lots of times!" He exclaimed.

Simply put, I told him, "Kareem, you have tremendously relevant experience. You need to polish your resume one more time and keep trying. You are eligible for an entry-level position in an HR department."

This sample is only an abbreviated version of the conversation, but you can see how I used his experiences to sell him on the idea that he was qualified for an HR position.

When you're job searching, you are the product, and your resume is the sales pitch. It's all about selling yourself to the company. Kareem followed my advice, landed an interview, and got the job. He was so grateful to me for "seeing" his potential when he couldn't see it himself. He became more confident, and within three months, he was promoted to a junior-level position in HR.

The key to sales is understanding what the customer wants. In order to do that, you need to understand yourself and what you have to offer. Take some time to think about your experiences, skills, and qualifications. What are your unique selling points? What sets you apart from the competition? Once you have a good understanding of what you offer, you can start selling yourself to prospective employers or other people in your life.

The Broken Mirror

In my house, I had a floor mirror that was broken. The frame was in good condition, but the glass was cracked. When I was moving out of my tiny apartment in NYC, I sold my furniture. Originally, I was planning to trash the mirror, but a friend who knew of my excellent marketing skills challenged me to sell it. I'm always up for a challenge, so I slapped a sticker on it for the ridiculous price of $150. However, the trick here wasn't that I was selling the mirror. I applied psychology and sold the metaphor behind the cracked glass and frame.

My sales pitch went as follows:

This mirror has been through a lot of shit—just like some of us. Alas, the mirror cracked under social pressure. However, it didn't shatter into pieces. The old mirror frame is elegant and gorgeous. The mirror can be easily detached from the frame and replaced, but I chose not to because the crack makes the mirror unique. It reminds me that beauty has no standards.

Within hours, I had a message from the Facebook Marketplace. The man laughed at me and said I was embarrassing myself. He said to delete the post because I would never sell "this piece of crap." Little did he know, within 24 hours I had five messages from people who were interested in the mirror. In fact, one woman hilariously negotiated prices with me, and we agreed on $70. That same evening, she appeared at my door with the cash in hand, ready to take the mirror with her. I gave her the mirror for free because I found her charming and wanted to pass along a good deed, but the moral of this story is that you can sell anything to anyone if you put your mind to it.

This broken mirror is a great example of how you can sell anything—you just need to find the right angle. That's what selling is all about—finding the right angle to present your product, idea, or service in a way that is appealing to your customer. Whether you're selling a physical product or an intangible service, the principles are the same. You need to understand what your customer wants and needs, and then present your offer in a way that is appealing to them.

Sharpen These Skills and You Will Be Unstoppable

If you can sharpen your psychology and sales skills, you will be unstoppable. These are essential skills that everybody should obtain and master throughout their lives. With these skills, you will understand what people want and need, and then present your offer in a way that appeals to them.

Reading is a fantastic way to learn psychology and build empathy. The books don't have to be directly related to psychology. Even fiction books can help you understand different points of view and empathize with people who think differently. You can also pick up textbooks or attend classes if you want to learn more about psychology in a structured way. Do whatever you have to.

Understand that the better you are at psychology and sales, the easier and more beneficial your life will be. These two skills are codependent, and you require both of them to be successful. Everything has a buyer. Everything is sellable. The ability to see what people want and then sell it to them is a skill that will always be in demand.

Don't wait until you need these skills to develop them. The earlier you start, the better off you will be. Start reading and practicing now so that when an opportunity comes knocking, you will be ready to take full advantage of it.

You should also follow your core values while developing your skills in psychology and sales. By being authentic and sticking to your values, you will build trust with the people you interact with. People can sense when you're being fake, and they will be turned off by it.

You should never, under any circumstance, sell something or utilize psychology skills if it will harm the person or bring any disadvantage to them. If it doesn't affect them at all besides being played, then go get something out of it—shoot for the stars. Otherwise, if it brings them any kind of negative consequence, it's not worth it, and you shouldn't do it. Look for an alternative solution.

Instead of Evening Prayers

1. Multi-level marketing companies and retail do a pretty good job with an introduction to sales training. If you can get exposed to these types of companies, take full advantage of them. Maybe take a summer or weekend job with one. They will teach basic sales tricks, plus you get paid.

2. Invest in nonprofessional psychology education. Read books, watch videos, listen to podcasts, or just observe people constantly. Never stop doing that. This skill can never be sharp enough.

6

FUCK NO!

You might think that the title of this chapter is a bit of a mouthful, but it's actually quite apt. In today's world, the word "no" is far too often used as a definitive answer instead of simply being the first step in a negotiation. In business, love, politics, or war... *no* should never be the last word.

So, what can you do when you're met with a big, fat *no*?

The answer is: Try everything you can to turn that *no* into a *yes*.

It might sound like a daunting task, but it's actually quite simple. All you need to do is use a little creativity, some persistence, and a lot of charm.

I was born and raised in Russia. The city I grew up in was in the middle of nowhere with a population of 17,000 or so people. It only had one college with one educational program, which is essentially the equivalent of an associate's degree in the US. In Russia, they have two types of associate programs: The entry-level one, which doesn't provide benefits for further education, and the pro-level one. This one is more complex and lets you skip the first two years of a bachelor's program if you decide to keep going.

The college I attended only offered a basic degree, and it was simply awful, with a poor reputation within the state. The acceptance rate was 100%, but the graduation rate was abysmal. Professors performed below the "I-don't-give-a-single-fuck" level, and students consumed liquor during the lectures at the back of the class. Nobody cared about anything. It was a Soviet ghetto.

I was an ambitious young boy, and this college was the only option available to me at the time. I survived somehow in the first year, but during the second one, I became depressed. The idea of wasting four years of my life at that place was killing me—especially without getting an excellent education and with no option to pursue my bachelor's degree in an expedited manner. I was in Hell.

One day, I came home early because two out of the four lectures had been canceled. That happened often, and it was the third time in a row. Annoyed and frustrated, I applied to different colleges within my state—one with a pro-level associate's program. One by one, I called all the accredited schools in my state to determine if they would accept me as a transferee and what their conditions were.

Every college greeted me with the same answer: "We don't accept transfers from entry-level programs. It's impossible. You would have to apply to the college and start from year one if accepted." After three hours of being greeted with the same answer, I reached the second to last college on my list. The receptionist similarly said they don't accept students from my college because it was part of a lame-ass program, but she also gave me a glimpse of hope. She said to call back the following Monday and speak to the principal about making arrangements.

I hung up feeling hopeful, although there was still a chance the principal would say, "No." Then I had a brilliant idea. Maybe it would be easier to negotiate and sell myself in person. At the time, I was 16 years old, and the college was 500 miles away from my home, but it was also my last hope for getting the fuck out of that godforsaken place.

Before leaving, I spoke to my mom. She was concerned about tuition, but I asked only for the bus fare. I was aiming to go to college for free. Reluctantly, she agreed, and Sunday morning, I was on my way. The following morning, I arrived at the principal's office. After listening carefully to my story, he replied, "No" with as much empathy as he could muster, but I refused to accept it.

"What would it take for me to get in?" I pleaded with the principal. Doubly, he replied that I needed to receive all the year-one credits, which were a lot. I was convinced, though, beyond a doubt, that I could do it. I would pass all the exams and receive all the grades before the semester was completed, as long as teachers were available.

His eyebrows raised at my response, and after a moment of silence, he told me I would still need to attend the ongoing classes, and only then would I be accepted—with unsubsidized tuition. I was glad to have a conditional "yes" finally, but I couldn't afford tuition. So, I started singing. It might sound random to you, and it certainly threw the principal for a loop, but I'm a talented singer and have taken part in singing competitions throughout my childhood. When I finished, the principal was confused and surprised at the same time. Before he could say anything, I started talking.

"I can sing. I will represent your college in every singing competition if you squeeze me in as a subsidized student." He was silent for a moment before finally saying, "Deal," but there was one more condition: My GPA. The principal said I couldn't get a grade lower than a B in any of my classes. If so, I would be transferred to the paid plan. We agreed, shook hands, and for the next three months, I barely slept. The result? I graduated from that college with honors before moving to Moscow, where I received my BA at a different university.

Always Try to Fight

The first step is to constantly try to fight. If you're met with a no, don't just accept it and move on. Instead, start by attempting to negotiate. See if there's any way that you can turn that no into a yes. If negotiation doesn't work, then try something else.

No harm comes from trying. If you don't succeed the first time, try again and again—and again if you have to. Eventually, you'll turn that no into a yes. Charm people into submission by using your wit, your humor, and your charisma to win them over. Oftentimes, all it takes is a little charm to get people to change their minds. Be persistent and never give up.

Try 1,001 Tactics Before Letting It Go

Yes, other people have boundaries, and we should respect the wishes of other people. Yes, our parents taught us not to be annoying, and a no is a no. Here's the thing: That doesn't mean that we should give up on what we want just because somebody else said *no*—we're not children dealing with our parents anymore. We deserve to make room and take up space in life. We deserve to get what we want, especially if we've worked hard for it.

If you want something badly enough, you need to try 1,001 different tactics before considering giving up. You need to be persistent and never take "no" for an initial answer. Again, consider my college story. I tried various avenues to get my point across, and honestly, I had even more prepared.

Remember, this goes back to our confidence and the two essential skills: Sales and psychology. If you want to be good at sales, you need to understand human psychology. You need to understand what motivates people and how to influence them. This knowledge will come in handy when you're trying to get somebody to say *yes*. It's part of their psychology to say *no*. Now you need to use your essential skills to get them to be open-minded and change their answer to *yes*.

Never give up. If you keep trying, eventually you will get what you want. Try different tactics and see what works. If one tactic doesn't work, move on to the next. Keep going until you find something that does work.

What we say isn't always important, but how we say it is. If you're having trouble getting somebody to say *yes*, try changing your approach. Try to be subtle instead of being aggressive or pushy. Instead of asking for a yes outright, try asking for a *maybe*. Be more flexible instead of demanding.

The key is to never give up—use all your psychology and sales tricks. If you really want something, you need to go the extra mile. You need to be relentless in your pursuit—show the importance and value of what you want.

No matter how many times you're met with a "no," don't give up. Continue to try new techniques, and eventually, you'll turn that *no* into a *yes*. Do what you can to set yourself apart from others. Consider my college story. I showed up in person instead of talking on the phone. I told my story from beginning to end and closed the argument by showcasing my talents. Giving up wasn't an option until I tried every single talent, every avenue, and even potentially embarrassed myself because my education was so important to me.

Pushing back against a "no" isn't just about getting what you want. It's also about respecting yourself. If you don't stand up for yourself, then you're essentially telling the other person that their opinion is more important than yours—that their *no* is more valid than your *yes*.

Don't let anyone tell you what you can and cannot do. If you want something, go out and get it. Let no one tell you that you're not good enough, because you are. You can achieve anything you set your mind to, as long as you're willing to fight for it. Of course, we should respect others' boundaries and their wishes, but that doesn't mean that we should give up on what we want.

If at first you don't succeed, try again. And again. And again. Until you finally get the *yes* that you've been fighting for.

Think Outside the Box

If you can't seem to win people over with your charm, then it's time to be innovative. Get creative and come up with an alternative approach. Sometimes, all it takes is a fresh perspective to get people to see the situation from your perspective, just like with me singing to the principal.

Be relentless in your pursuit of a *yes*. Don't be afraid to use your talents or even embarrass yourself. If someone tells you "no," don't take it personally. Instead, use it as motivation to try even harder. You can achieve anything you set your mind to, as long as you're willing to fight for it. So, go out there and get what's yours. Remember: No is not an answer; it's simply the first step in a negotiation.

Do everything in your power to win. Only if you have tried everything, and you still don't receive a yes, then let it go. Of course, we are not magicians or dictators. We cannot make everyone accept our terms and have the world fall in line with our visions. In the end, a *no* is still a *no*. We should always remember and respect people's decisions. However, until we have truly done everything in our power to turn that *no* into a *yes*, we should never give up. We always have to fight to the end and be confident that "no" is the only answer.

Be Firm and Offer Resolutions

A great tactic to employ when trying to get someone to say "yes" is to be firm and highlight the benefits of receiving what you want. When you're assertive, be clear about what you want and why you deserve it. You need to make a strong case for yourself. You are the lawyer of your life. In order to win, you need to build a powerful and convincing argument.

Furthermore, when you're assertive, it's also important to offer resolutions. This means that you need to have a plan B and C ready. You need to be prepared for any objection that the other person might throw your way. You need to offer solutions to any problems that might arise. This shows that you're not only assertive but also resourceful and capable.

Lastly, when you're assertive, it's important to be confident. Remember, confidence is key. You need to believe in yourself and your ability to get what you want. If you don't believe in yourself, then nobody else will.

For example, let's say that you're trying to get a raise at work. In this case, you would need to sit down with your boss and explain why you deserve a raise. You would need to be clear about what you want and build a strong case for yourself. Maybe you deserve the raise because you've been with the company for a long time or because you've taken on extra assignments. Maybe once you receive the raise, you'll be able to work even harder and contribute even more to the company. Whatever the case may be, you need to make a convincing argument for yourself. You need to articulate it clearly and confidently.

Furthermore, you would also need to offer resolutions. What if your boss says *no*? What if your boss says that he can't give you a raise right now, but he can give you a bonus? What if your boss says that he can give you a raise, but it won't be as much as you want? You need to be prepared for any objection that your boss might throw your way. You need to have a solution ready for every problem. Maybe you could offer to lead a new project or take on additional responsibilities. Show that you're willing to go the extra mile in order to get what you want.

Lastly, remember to be confident. Stand your ground and be clear about what you want. You don't want to come across as angry or unreasonable though. We're trying to influence people here, not antagonize them.

Apply Honey Before Spanking

Have you heard of the saying, "You catch more flies with honey than with vinegar?" This is true in life as well. If you're constantly fighting and arguing with people, you will not get very far. If you're sweet and charming, people are more likely to be open to hearing what you have to say.

Of course, this doesn't mean that you should take "no" for an answer. You should still fight for what you want. However, try using honey before resorting to spanking. You may be surprised at how well it works. Be soft and gentle when you negotiate, and then you can start to get more forceful if needed. Try to win the person over by being reasonable. For instance, if you're trying to get a raise at work, don't just demand more money. Instead, explain why you deserve it and how extra appreciation can elevate you.

You can do this by prompting empathy from the other person. Ask them to put themselves in your shoes and see the situation from your viewpoint. For instance, in the case of wanting a raise, you could tell them about all of your greatest achievements at the company, the value you've brought, and ask them how they would feel if they were in the same position. Wouldn't they want their hard work to be appreciated? Kindness is a more effective strategy to get what you want than outright demanding it. Be nice to them and try to get them to understand your wants and needs.

However, if that doesn't work, get tougher. Keep getting tougher as much as you can within legal and moral boundaries until they do what you want. Start by being sweet like honey and slowly become more assertive as you utilize your negotiation tactics.

There's nothing wrong with being assertive and fighting for what you want. In fact, it's admirable. So, don't be afraid to go out and get what you deserve. You're not being unreasonable by asking for it. If you don't get it, don't give up. Keep trying, and eventually, you'll get the *yes* that you've been fighting for.

The point is, never give up. If you want something badly enough, you need to be willing to fight for it. No matter how many times you're met with a "no," don't give up. Continue to try new strategies.

The next time you're met with a "no," don't despair. Remember that it's not the end of the world, and with a little perseverance, you'll find a way to get what you want.

Don't Be Afraid to Appear Rude

We live in a society where we're taught to be polite and respectful at all times. In fact, far too often, we're told to bite our tongues and not say what we're really thinking. However, sometimes being rude is the best course of action. Sometimes, in order to get what you want, you need to go against the grain. You may need to appear rude or impolite if that's what it takes. Of course, as said above, start with a little honey; when that doesn't work, turn to spanking.

For instance, let's say you missed your connecting flight because the first flight was delayed. You know you deserve to be compensated, but they're refusing to do it to you. Most people would just suffer in silence and hope that the situation would improve. However, if you want to get what you desire—in this case, compensation for your missed flight—you need to speak up. You might have to be rude. Customer Service usually wouldn't give you much unless you went ape-shit on them.

Of course, there's a fine line between being assertive and being outright rude. You don't want to be so impolite that you're offensive or make enemies. However, you don't want to be a doormat, either. Balance is crucial.

If you're in a situation where you're not getting what you want, sometimes it's best to be bold and direct. Don't be afraid to speak your mind and tell it like it is. You may not make friends this way, but you will get what you want. If you need something, remember that it's all about you. You have to get it done.

Negotiate Often and Do Your Homework

One of my first jobs in America wasn't well paid. It's hard to get a job without prior experience, and when your English is not sufficient, so I took a shitty office job. The owner of the company hired inexperienced immigrants, so she wouldn't have to pay them much. I'm not judging them here. It's capitalism. Everyone chooses their own survival methods and level of morality and values, but it was the reason I could pick up the job.

Anyway, two months into the position, I asked for a raise, and the company said, "yes." They gave me an extra $2,000 a year. Another two months passed, and I returned with the same request. They gave me another $2,000. Two months passed again, and I asked for another raise. This time, they said, "no." If you haven't figured it out by now, of course, I wasn't planning on accepting that without a fight.

I was prepared and pulled out the homework that I had put together before showing up. I revealed my impeccable attendance chart, my amazing performance numbers, glowing customer reviews, gratitude emails from coworkers, and the median salary for the same position in the area, which was higher than my current salary. The low starting salary for the new hires was a strategy I understood. I understood they were creating room for raises for driven employees, and that's why I kept negotiating. I knew my skill set had improved to the point where I met market expectations and other companies would love to have me on board.

However, I appreciate loyalty, and I try to return it myself. That's why I gave them a chance to pay me reasonable compensation for the work I do. I left their office with a $5,000 raise. That brought me to the average market compensation for the role. Some people may think that every two months is way too often to ask for a raise. In some cases, yes. However, evaluate each situation on a case-by-case basis. In my case, I was underpaid. The politics behind the owner's policy were to hire inexperienced coworkers for a low salary, train them, and keep the salary increase as slow as possible. I knew my value, and I knew I deserved the pay I asked for. I was reasonable and realistic. Do your homework, negotiate, and be bold but reasonable. Don't take the first "no" as the only answer.

I wanted to bring you a concrete example from the consumer world when a company messes something up and is not helpful, but I have way too many to choose from—not to mention, most of them are honestly kind of the same. Your food delivery tastes disgusting, your package is missing, your return is lost on the way, your hotel has issues, etc. In every case, the answer from Customer Service is almost always no, or they can't do anything about it. However, if you don't give up and continue to ask questions, most of the time you'll get what you want in the end.

Sometimes companies are accommodating, but they will still do their best to minimize their losses. Often, they are not even willing to help you out or solve the issue they have created. What I would always do is nicely explain what happened and what I've been through because of those circumstances (honey). I try to seek empathy, which can be a secret weapon among humans. There are genuinely nice people who will try to help you out if you can elicit an emotional response politely.

If you are not happy with the resolution, reasonably negotiate. However, sometimes it doesn't help, and they won't fix it. In that case, despite all the hate toward Karens—become the worst one. If honey doesn't work, do some spanking. Talk to as many supervisors as you need. Be annoying. Get what they owe you. Ring your bells everywhere—phone support, chat support, email support, Twitter, Facebook—climb up the corporate ladder. Believe me, if they really messed up and you are not a bullshitter, 99% of the time, it will work. You will get what you deserve. Negotiate, and never settle for less than you think you deserve.

Instead of Evening Prayers

1. Analysis at work: Think about a time when you expected a *yes* but got a *no*. Is there a tactic you could have tried to make that become a *yes*? If so, why didn't you try that approach? What caused your hesitation? Can you work on those strategies, so next time you will start fighting against the *no*?

2. Promise yourself, from now on to never take "no" as an official ruling unless it is not worth the time.

7

— . —

GARBAGE COLLECTOR

As humans, we have an incessant need to hold on to objects, even if they no longer serve us. We become attached to material possessions, people, and even experiences that no longer make us happy. Then, instead of letting them go, we become what I like to call "garbage collectors." We hold on to things that are no longer beneficial to us, thinking that we may need them in the future. However, the truth is, those objects are just weighing us down.

The Buddhists believed that the root of all suffering is attachment, and I believe that to be true. When we are attached to anything, we become attached to the idea of it. When that attachment is taken away or we lose it, we suffer. We hold on to objects or people because we think they will make us happy, but in reality, they don't bring us any positive long-term value. Let go of what no longer serves you. It's time to let go of the people who don't bring you joy. It's time to let go of the experiences that were sold to you as necessities for your bucket list.

Simplify Your Life

Life is hard and complicated, but mostly because we make it that way. We fill our lives with so many things that we don't really need or want, such as having a closet with 20 pairs of shoes or buying another jacket because it was on sale. Then we wonder why we're so unhappy and stressed out.

Simplifying your life is a great way to improve yourself. The more possessions you have, the more complicated and stressful your life becomes. If you can get rid of the unnecessary and unimportant objects in your life, you'll be surprised at how much simpler and happier your life will become.

Clear up the space around you and the space within you. You will feel lighter. You will become a fluffy white cloud that can easily travel from place to place—physically, mentally, and spiritually. Every piece of garbage you hold makes you heavier, creates obligations, and occupies space within yourself. Fill yourself up with something more pleasant—a person or experience that makes you feel alive and happy.

Stop hanging on to items that you don't need or want. If it doesn't make you happy, get rid of it. It's as simple as that. You don't need a lot of stuff to be happy. You only need the basics. In fact, the more stuff you have, the more stressed and unhappy you're likely to be. Get rid of the stuff that's weighing you down and keeping you from being light. A life filled with love, joy, happiness, peace, and simplicity is a life well-lived. Start simplifying your life today and see how much it can elevate your spirit.

Always try to choose experiences over objects or material possessions. People and purchases will come and go, but experiences will stay with you forever. Instead of buying a new car or clothes, go on a vacation. Spend your money on experiences instead of possessions—it will be more fulfilling in the long run. If someone asks you what you want for your birthday, Christmas, or anniversary and you don't need anything, ask for an experience gift. Maybe you can receive a voucher for a cooking class or go on a retreat.

Don't bet your happiness on external values such as goals like a new car, a bigger house, or a promotion at work. These are wonderful goals and can bring momentary happiness, but it won't last. It's a sad truth, but most physical items are either necessities or will only bring simple and momentary pleasure.

Material possessions become the root of all your desires. Experiences are better alternatives. Focus on experiences that will create lasting memories, such as learning a new skill, going on an adventure, or taking up a new hobby. Look for the extrinsic value that leads you to happiness because joy based on external stimuli has a short mood-boosting period.

Consider this argument: When you're old, do you think you'll be looking back on your life and saying, "I'm so glad I had a nice car"? No, you'll be thinking about the experiences you had and the people you shared them with. Don't worry about filling your home with pretty objects or having a garage full of cars to use—worry about experiencing life. In your last days, you will not regret the purchases you didn't make or the people you didn't impress.

If you regret not impressing anyone, it'll be your damn self. You'll be longing for the places that you never visited and the risks that you never took. Even if you bought your dream car, make sure it's a tool that enhances the experiences in your life. Instead of having just the car, wouldn't it be much more thrilling to think about all the amazing road trips you took with people you love driving the car you love? So, get out there and start living your life to the fullest!

Possessions

We live in a society that tells us we need to have a lot of possessions in order to be happy or to be viewed as successful. However, while having more might make you seem better well-off, it also gives you more to worry about. The more possessions you have, the more you will experience loss. The more you have, the more you are a slave to something other than yourself.

The more "things" or possessions you own, the more you have to take care of. The more you own, the more your mind is occupied with thoughts of those objects—your brain becomes more cluttered. Mobility is a challenge when you have many possessions. You're polluting your space. If your space is cluttered, it's harder to breathe (physically and metaphorically) and tougher to be creative.

Consider this: The heavier the load, the slower the car drives, and the more it consumes gas. Or think of a hot air balloon—the lighter the load, the higher it flies.

You, as a person, want to fly high, be fast, efficient, creative, and free. All the garbage you own slows you down and takes up space for your creativity. The less you own, the better. This concept is one that you feel rather than see. The shorter your maintenance list is—the less stressed and occupied you are. Do not collect garbage because you spent money on it or someone gifted it to you and you feel bad about trashing it. If you don't need or like something, get rid of it.

I'm 100% sure you have items strewn about your home that you don't need but plan to keep. Check your closet. Are there any outfits you don't remember wearing recently? Ask yourself this: if I didn't wear it in the past six months, will I wear it in the next six months? How often would I wear it, and is it worth the space?

Check your drawers. Are there holiday cards from your ex-coworkers, neighbors, or third cousins? Do you care about those? Not really? Then trash them. When you clear up your space, you will feel relieved, light, and enthusiastic about new opportunities you have space for.

For example, I never purchase new clothing until I get rid of an old piece first. Mostly, I prefer to sell because the internet is a wonderful opportunity to access various marketplaces. In just a few clicks, you can find several platforms and list your item. Then the person picks it up, or you ship it off, and you receive your pay. Easy-peasy.

Personally, I don't keep birthday cards, postcards, or letters. I don't want it in my space if it's not a functional item. If it doesn't serve a purpose, it's garbage. If I care about the sender and it has sentimental value, I snap a picture for memories before trashing it. For souvenirs, that's a whole other story.

I detest cheap-ass souvenirs such as fridge magnets, small statues, or those weird, collectible spoons. What can I even use those for? I told all my friends—if you want to bring me a souvenir from your adventure, bring something useful, authentic, and local. If they're going to Mexico, I tell them to bring me a handmade lamp, a pot, or spicy candy that I can't find anywhere else. If they're going to Brazil, bring a bag of coffee. Going to Ukraine? Bring me back a bottle of Ukrainian liquor that I can't find here. You get the idea, right?

The bottom line is that if the item doesn't provide necessary help or create an experience and you don't love it, get rid of it. If you do not wear it, eat it, or drink it, get rid of it. Don't be a garbage collector. You don't need that in your life. To me, even books are dust collectors—ironic considering I'm writing a book for you to read. However, if I know I won't read the book again, I won't keep it. I'll give it to the library or a friend to read. Simple. I've got an e-reader, and I'm not impartial to screen reading. It's more eco-friendly, cheaper, and I can keep an entire library within the device.

Furniture is the same. With too much furniture, a house looks like a museum. Your chair turns into the closet, the floor is a maze, and you can never find your keys. Fewer pieces of quality furniture that you absolutely love rather than a bunch of cheap shit that you'll have to replace in a few years is a lot better. The less furniture you have, the more freeing it is.

The goal is to own as little as possible while still being comfortable. If the furniture isn't used appropriately within the home, I don't keep it. Think about all the time and money you spend on maintaining your possessions. The price isn't the only concern; there's also the time you spend cleaning it, fixing it, and worrying about it.

The possessions you have should make you happy. If they don't, get rid of them! You don't need that kind of negativity in your life. Life is too short to keep objects you don't need or love. Be ruthless with what you allow into your space.

Experiences

Being a garbage collector isn't only about the things we keep and collect in our homes. Although I believe experiences are better than material objects, sometimes we hold on to the experiences we have or wish to have. There are certain types of experiences I know

I don't want, and I will not engage in them just because other people are doing them or because they're considered "must-dos."

I'm also not going to visit places because they're popular or "trendy." Experiences such as bungee jumping, cage diving with sharks, or any other type of "thrilling" activity don't appeal to me. Only certain thrills are joyful to me. I will not do an activity or visit a place just to say I did it and post a picture on social media. That's not living—that's called FOMO (Fear Of Missing Out), and trust me, you're not missing out on anything.

I've seen people apply their attachment to experiences often. In fact, I've done it myself. Bucket lists are a perfect example. Have you seen a headline for an article like "Places to Visit Before You Die," "Must Read Books for 20-year-olds," "Movies You Can't Miss," "The Bucket List for the Ultimate Adventurer," or "Top 30 TV Shows Everybody Should Watch"? All these bucket lists are opinions, wishes, desires, or sales pitches from someone else.

These are simply societal pressures used to accomplish massive goals and visit the world, but why? Do we need to fit everyone's opinions into ourselves before we die? What happens if we don't make it to those places or do those activities? Will our lives be any less complete? I want to encourage you not to fall into this social trap.

I'm not saying don't travel or have experiences. By all means, please do, because those are learning experiences. However, be picky about the experiences you have and choose activities you truly want to do. Don't decide based solely on some arbitrary list or what's popular. Only engage in activities that you are interested in and excited about. If it doesn't pique your interest, then it's not worth your time or money. Popularity or trendiness isn't sufficient reasoning to allow yourself to be pressured into activities that don't suit you. You don't have to take part in what everybody else is doing. You can be different, and that's okay.

You don't have to join the internet rat race and follow bucket lists created by someone else. You don't have to go skydiving because it's the top activity to do on your friend's bucket list. If you are not seeking a thrill or looking to broaden your comfort zone, don't fucking do it. If you've never watched *Friends* and you don't really feel like watching it, don't feel left out because millions of people love the show.

Visiting all 50 states because you want to impress people is unnecessary and a waste of time. You don't have to go across the globe to post a picture from the other side, like everyone else you know. Attending every single Christmas tree installation to experience the "holidays in NYC in full capacity" is unnecessary. Instead, be a part of the process, be present, and do what you actually want to.

By maximizing everything to the extreme and trying to experience it all, you are not actually experiencing the tasks themselves. You are experiencing the completion of them. You become a runner who's trying to complete a marathon to get some type of recognition—not enjoying the high. The question is: From whom are you trying to get recognition? Is it yourself? I doubt that. You want to impress others by collecting garbage experiences. Save your time and money. Do what you truly want to do. Don't become the woman in the story I'm about to share.

A coworker of mine, Crystal, had the goal of visiting every country in the world. It sounds like an impressive achievement, right? At the time we spoke, she had visited over 50 countries, which is a wonderful feat. However, when I picked her brain about her goals and travels, I concluded that Crystal wasn't traveling to those countries because she wanted to learn more about their culture or because she enjoyed traveling. She traveled because she wanted a "traveler's" title—the title of being someone who stepped foot in every country. It was just something she thought would be cool to do—FOMO trips.

She didn't truly experience those places because all she cared about was visiting as many places as possible and checking them off her list. She was a grown woman following someone else's bucket list. When she was ready, she would pick a flight with extended layovers in different countries. The moment she stepped foot in a country, that was a "visit." In two days, she visited three countries because she jumped between major (a.k.a. Instagramable) sites to take pictures before progressing to the next destination.

Honestly, I felt sorry for her. To me, she looked like a rat chasing a race around the world. Her idea of being cool was to impress society by literally stepping foot in every single country—even if it was only for a few minutes. Her entire personality was built upon proving to the world that she was well-traveled. When meeting new people and presenting elevator pitches, she never forgot to mention how many countries she'd visited.

It shaped how she saw the world, and it was all garbage because if you asked her what those experiences had brought upon her, she would stumble. For her, it wasn't the experience, the joy, or even the destinations. Her focus was on the number and receiving the "world traveler" title to impress others.

Don't do that to yourself. Do not become like Crystal. You shouldn't collect experiences just for the sake of it. Life is too short to live someone else's version of it. Invest your precious time and money in fulfillment. Collect experiences that inspire passion in yourself. Be around people who you want to be around, and try activities that make you feel good.

In the end, it is not about how many places you visited or how many goals you achieved. Were those experiences worth your time, money, and energy? Did they improve the quality of your life? You don't need to visit every single country to be cool. You shouldn't even worry about appearing cool to others. Live for the love of the experience.

Instead of going to Paris for a few hours just to snap a picture, go to Paris to experience a proper French breakfast with a spectacular view of the Eiffel Tower. Enjoy the fresh smell of espresso and savor the taste of butter croissants. Instead of going on a safari because your friends think it's cool, go on a safari because you have always wanted to see wild elephants. Go zip lining through the Amazon rainforest or learn how to surf in Hawaii if those experiences intrigue you.

Engage in activities that will leave you with happy memories and stories to tell and that will make you feel more alive—not just experiences that put a check-mark next to something on a list. This is your life, so live it for yourself. If you're not living for yourself, you are collecting garbage.

People

Some people can also be garbage, and just like how you would throw away garbage, you should also get rid of the toxic people in your life. Whether it is a romantic relationship, a friendship, or even a family member, if they don't enhance the positivity in your life, then they need to be gone. Life is too short to keep people around who only bring you down.

This doesn't mean you should only associate your-self with people who are wealthy, popular, or always happy. Surround yourself with people who make you feel good, inspire you to be better, and support your goals—people who add value to your life.

Not everyone is going to be like that, and that's okay. You don't need a lot of friends, though. That's the point—just a few close ones who you can trust and rely on. Otherwise, we pollute ourselves with people we don't need. Sometimes we collect people because we want to be popular, needed, and in demand. That is another mental trap. We either want to show the world how cool we are by having so many friends, or we want to prove something to ourselves, such as that we're likable and a good person. Or sometimes, we do this to cover insecurities or trauma we've endured.

Maybe a person wasn't popular during their childhood, and now they are trying to catch up by having as many friends as possible in their adult lives. Or perhaps they feel insecure about themselves, so they are trying to compensate for the gaps by having cool people around.

Another major reason we collect people we don't need is because we feel invested in them. This is a mental trap as well, which we'll speak about more in another chapter. But for now, you should know that it doesn't matter how long you've known the person, how close you were, or how much time and energy you've put into the relationship. If it's not working anymore, then let it go. Don't collect people you don't enjoy.

A sense of security is another reason we choose to keep people around us, even if we don't really like them. This often happens in romantic relationships, where people stay together even though they are unhappy because they are afraid of being alone. They would rather be with someone—anyone—than by themselves. While it is normal to feel anxious about being single, it is not healthy to stay in a relationship just for the sake of being in one.

It's another trap formed by your mind! If you find yourself in a situation like this, remember that you are not alone. There are plenty of people out there who would love to be in a relationship with you. However, more importantly, love being by yourself first and foremost. Only then will you be able to find the right person for you.

Don't keep someone around just because they could be possibly useful to you. The need may never arise, and it probably never will, but you will keep investing your time and energy in those people. So, drop it. Never keep boring, toxic, or sad people around. Clear your space.

Food

Do you know how much food we waste every day? One reason we waste so much food is that we're not eating what we really want. We're eating what we think we should eat or what's convenient. I've seen it happen so many times. People eat a meal they don't like because they have already spent money on it, and they don't want it to be a waste.

Or, they would take leftovers, knowing for sure they would never eat them at home. Some people shovel in the food because it's free or discounted—even if they're not hungry. They buy too much food, thinking with their eyes or stomachs, only for it to end up in the garbage. Remember one thing—your stomach is not a garbage can. Your body is a temple—the most precious and the most expensive one.

Put nothing in your body that you don't enjoy. You don't like the food you ordered? Return it. Ask for something else. Is it impossible to return? Then, trash that shit, and don't look back. You paid for a refillable cup and feel like you need to get another round of soda to get the most bang for your buck. Dude, don't embarrass yourself. If you are not thirsty for another cup of soda, be done with it.

Digital Space

Our physical and mental spaces aren't the only areas that can get cluttered. Organizing our digital spaces is also crucial. This means getting rid of unused or unnecessary documents or apps that take up space on your computer or phone. This includes old files, photos, apps, and even social media.

Social media can wreak havoc on our self-esteem if we're not careful. If you are someone who compulsively checks their social media accounts, you may have noticed that scrolling through your feed can sometimes leave you feeling worse when you stop than when you started. Much of what we see on social media is not an accurate representation of reality. People only post the highlights of their lives, which can make us compare our own lives to what we see and feel like we're falling short. So, if you find social media is causing you more harm than good, it may be time to take a break from it or even delete your account altogether.

You don't have to follow or be friends with people on social media because you know them or because you met them once at a party. Keep your feed clean and fresh. If something is boring or irritating to you, just unfollow/unfriend it. Your digital space affects your mental health. It's a proven fact, and I'm sure you feel it. Follow people you like. Follow pages that bring you joy and/or knowledge. Never feel obligated to interact if you don't want to.

The same goes for anything else that is taking up space on your computer or phone. If you don't use it, get rid of it. If it's taking up space and causing you anxiety, delete it. Your digital space should reflect your physical space. Keep only what is necessary and what brings you joy.

Keep your devices fresh and organized. Delete all the apps you don't use, organize your photo albums and delete duplicates and screenshots you don't need, plus the millions of boring selfies you couldn't decide on. Don't keep your electronics messy. When it comes to your phone, tablet, and laptop—keep everything neat. It will reflect on your mental state as well.

Keep your online presence clean and fresh. Google your name and see what pops up. If there is any information about yourself that you don't want to appear online, either delete it or reach out to the company holding the data about you and demand they remove it. If someone Googled you, they should see only what you want them to see. Your digital self should align with the way you portray yourself in the real world.

Also, I would recommend creating and following a digital hygiene routine. Don't keep sensitive info like your full legal name, full date of birth, phone number, and addresses online. You never know who might use it or how. It's better to be safe than sorry. Also, as a quick public announcement: Coworkers usually aren't your friends. Keep that in mind. The only social media I allow my coworkers to see is LinkedIn. Everything else is private.

Coworkers shouldn't be able to find you on social media, and it's not a good idea for them to know about your personal life. This connection could cause conflicts of interest, so keep your coworkers away from your intimate life. Your coworkers should be extremely far from your persona.

Memories and Thoughts

Think of your mind as a filing cabinet or a room in your house. If it's cluttered and messy, it's going to be hard to find what you're looking for, and it's going to be harder to focus on what's important. In this cabinet, we keep our thoughts, beliefs, and memories. Some people like to dig into their memory pile often. Others push away memories—both good and bad.

Regardless, if the cabinet is organized and clean, you'll be able to find what you need quickly and easily, and you'll be able to focus on what's important. Of course, this is easier said than done. However, your thoughts and memories should be cleaned and organized. You shouldn't hold on to shitty memories that bring you pain. Don't hold on to thoughts that make you uneasy.

To do this, you must first notice your thoughts, distortions, and unhelpful self-talk. Start by spotting the moments you think about something useless or negative. If you hold some memories that are not positive, don't return to them often. Dreadful memories are part of your journey and your experience. You can't erase them, and you shouldn't, but you also shouldn't keep them on the "memory shelf" within close proximity. Keep them somewhere in the back. Let them be there, but not too close to the surface.

Second, practice accepting that these thoughts are just thoughts and not reality. You might think or feel a certain way, but that doesn't mean that it's genuine and accurate. Then, practice letting go of these thoughts. Your memories and thoughts should make you feel good. They should bring a smile to your face or make you laugh. They should make you feel happy, loved, and supported. If they don't, put them away as far as possible, like in a back room or further on the shelf. You don't need them. Clear up space on the handy shelves for something more healthy, useful, inspirational, or good.

This is your life, and you get to choose what goes in it. Fill your life with happiness, inspiration, and growth. Don't be afraid to let go of what doesn't accomplish that.

Do not become a garbage collector. Do not NUMB your life down by only doing what others perceive to be fun or because everyone else is doing it. You are not a trash can. You are not meant to hold on to objects that do not serve you. You are meant to live a life that is authentic to yourself. Find what is important to you and let go of the hindrances that are holding you back.

Instead of Evening Prayers

1. Do an inventory of your home and get rid of what you don't need, use, or enjoy. It's your choice how to dispose of them: Garage sale, donation, or trash.

2. Clean your social media by unfollowing people or muting whoever doesn't spark joy on your feed. Delete people and photos of others you do not care about or communicate with regularly.

3. Organize your apps and delete the ones you don't need or use. Do the same with your camera roll. Delete duplicate images, screenshots, and selfies from all your electronic devices. Make it easy to navigate all your programs,

reducing wasteful time and confusion. Check your online presence everywhere, including search engines, and delete unwanted information from online resources or request the company that holds the data to do so.

4. Do you have a bucket list, must-watch TV shows, movies, or must-read books? Audit and turn them into your own personal must-read or watch list. You can look to others for ideas or inspirations, but only pick what you want to do, not what some schmuck said you should.

5. Think about the people you interact with. Are you really enjoying their company or feel forced to hang around them? Think about your exit strategy. Are you ready to cut them off? What does that scene look like, and what do you really feel about cutting them out of your world?

6. When you are old, would you regret the possessions you didn't buy or the people you didn't impress? How about places you didn't go?

8

— ◦ —

BANANA SPLIT

When I was about two years old, my parents separated. My father cheated on my mother, and she refused to forgive him, so they split up. That was their business. They were two consenting adults, and they both decided that their relationship was no longer working for them. I didn't judge my father for his adultery—not my sin or my business.

As a result, my father wasn't involved much in my life and never supported us. I grew up in the '90s, and we lived in the middle of nowhere in Russia. Times were tough—no jobs, famine, etc. My father, however, was better off than us. When I was about six years old, I was walking home from singing classes on a Saturday morning—a market day in our small town. I saw my father walking from the market and toward me. In his right hand, he held a bunch of bananas. However, when he saw me walking toward him, he flicked his wrist backward, attempting to hide the bunch behind the length of his forearm.

He thought I would not notice the bananas he was trying to hide in his hand. I was embarrassed to even be associated with the situation and to have a dad who couldn't share a goddamn banana with his child. I was embarrassed that this happened when my mom and I were struggling and would've appreciated a simple yet deliciously ripe banana. With all those emotions swirling within me, I played his game and pretended not to see the bananas.

I tried not to glance at his hand. Instead, I smiled and asked how he was doing before rushing away from him. It wasn't until I reached the comfort and safety of my home that I broke into tears. The brain of a child couldn't understand such behavior from an adult. No reasonable explanation existed. It didn't matter how hard I tried to answer all the questions running through my mind—the situation made little sense to my six-year-old mind.

I concluded that there was no explanation for it in my reality, and that's when I realized that it's not always possible to justify people's actions. People do crazy shit, and sometimes they don't even understand why they do what they do. When someone does something that makes little sense to us, all we can do is walk away. Confronting those people or trying to understand their reasoning is pointless. We don't need to figure out their reasoning or give them a chance to explain themselves. We don't owe them anything. Just walk away and live your life the way you want to live it, according to your own values.

That day was the last day I was affiliated with my father. I refused to see him ever again, and you know what? It was the best decision I ever made because I learned some people are just not worth our time and energy. We don't need to explain ourselves to them or try to make them see reason. Just walk away, as I did, and never look back. That's what I call a banana split. No confrontations, no talks, just conclusions and moving on.

The Irish Exit

The Irish exit might not be the most elegant way to handle a situation, but it is effective. By the time I learned about the phrase "Irish exist," I'd already experienced it. The "banana split" is my version of the Irish exit. The Irish exit is when you just leave without saying goodbye. You don't make a scene, you don't explain yourself, you just walk away.

Think of it this way: You attend a party, and you have a great time. After a couple of hours, you decide it's time to go home because you're just not feeling it anymore. The music is too loud, the people are too drunk, and you're exhausted. Some people go around and say their goodbyes, giving everyone a kiss on the cheek and telling them how much fun they had.

However, what if you don't want to make a scene? What if you just want to leave quietly and with no fanfare? That's when you do the Irish exit. You simply slip out the door, telling no one where you're going. You don't say goodbye, you don't thank your host, and you don't make any false promises to stay in touch. You just disappear into the night. Now, to some, this might seem like an impolite way to handle the situation, but sometimes it's the best way. The Irish exit is a great way to avoid confrontations and awkward goodbyes. It also helps you preserve your energy. When you're ready to leave, you just leave. You don't waste any time or effort saying goodbye. You just go.

The Irish exit is the best way to handle situations when you're just not feeling it anymore. Whether you're at a party, meeting, date, or even a hook-up, if you're ready to leave, just leave. You don't have to explain yourself or make any promises. You don't owe anyone anything.

Sometimes it's the best option you have. I've used the Irish exit many times in my life. My goodbyes are my forgiveness. It's a way of cutting ties and moving on. We've all been hurt by someone in our lives and sometimes, the best way to deal with that hurt is to just walk away. To leave without looking back. If someone does something that doesn't align with your values or if someone mistreats you, just walk away. They're not worth your time or energy.

If the situation is beyond fucked up, and I don't see any reason to save that person in my eyes—I don't justify them or their actions. Understanding them is unnecessary. I never confront. I don't analyze. Furthermore, I throw them overboard and move on. That's what I call a banana split: No confrontations or talks—only conclusions and moving on. I'm not saying that the Irish exit is the best way to handle every situation, but sometimes, it's the best way to handle a fucked-up situation.

It's a way of preserving your energy and your sanity. This goes back to Chapter 1. No one has to give a fuck about you, and if they show you they don't care about you, especially in a nasty way, just walk away. You're better than that. You're worth more than that and deserve better than that. So, the next time you find yourself in a situation where you're just not feeling it, just walk away. Do the Irish exit—be a banana split.

Instead of Evening Prayers

1. Analysis at work: Think about a situation of severe mistreatment. What came to mind after the shock? Did you try to analyze it, thinking it might have been your fault? Did you confront the person and ask for an explanation? I bet you did not get any concrete reasoning or a satisfactory answer. It is probably still a mystery. Why would this person act that way? So, if anything like that ever happens again, would you waste precious resources to overanalyze again? Answer this once and remember it for the rest of your life.

9

— · —

STABBING THE PUPPY

My friend, Lena, is a beautiful human being. She's caring and empathetic, and she has many great human qualities. I value her a lot. However, she has one quality that I'm not a fan of: She doesn't know how to control or hold her liquor. When she drinks, she becomes aggressive and turns into a completely different being. She doesn't drink often, so that's not the problem. The problem is who she becomes when she does take a sip.

Now, we're adults here, and I'm in no position to tell an adult how to live their life, especially someone I value. She's aware of the problem and works on it in her own way. However, within the first year of our friendship, she invited me to a birthday party where she got drunk and started acting out. I'll spare you the details because it was a bunch of nasty nonsense. Nonetheless, the party ended for me after she approached me that evening, completely irritated by my enjoyment of the party, and nastily told me to leave. So, I did.

Two days later, someone told her about the incident at the party, and she sincerely apologized. I comforted her and appreciated the apology, but I never forgave her and never will. I'm not holding a grudge, and I don't treat her any differently. We still hang out occasionally; as I said, she's a sweet person, but I learned my lesson. I'm never around Lena if there's alcohol involved, and I forgive no one for anything.

Banana Splits Can Be Reserved

In Chapter 8, we spoke about banana splits and the Irish exit. Sometimes ditching people without saying goodbye is the best way to handle disrespectful or shady behavior. On the same note, though, sometimes cutting people off completely isn't the best way to handle a problem. I want to be clear: I don't think people who make mistakes should be punished forever. My suggestion isn't to break up with every person who's wronged you—in a big or small way.

I'm a firm believer in second chances. However, certain actions, like aggression, only get one mistake. I don't need or want to see that person again in that state. Some situations are still serious, but not as fucked up as a banana split scenario. In those situations, I think it's best to give someone a second chance. You don't have to forgive, and especially don't forget, but you can give someone a second chance. Just be wary and don't let them pull the same shit twice.

Don't Forget

Forgive and forget is a common saying for a reason. Holding on to anger and resentment can lead to long-term problems. However, that doesn't mean you have to forget what happened. We have short memory spans and cool off easily, which can lead us to step into the same pile of dog shit again. I think remembering the pain someone has caused you is crucial to your mental health. That way, if they ever try to do it again, you'll be more likely to catch it early on and nip it in the bud.

I'm a strong antagonist of drama. I think life's too short to be angry with people. However, I also believe this means applying the "never forget" rule to serious shit. If someone has done something that's really hurtful, make sure you never forget what they did. In my case, Lena was disrespectful and crossed a line. If I see her drinking, I know to hightail it out of there.

Disregard human mistakes and misunderstandings because we're human and no one is perfect. If someone did something to you non-intentionally or by mistake, please don't harp on anger or disappointment. For instance, if a friend was venting to you about their day and they said something that unintentionally hurt your feelings, talk to them about it. They'll understand and learn from it. We all make mistakes. Instead, focus on the people who have acted with bad intentions.

If someone disrespects you on purpose or intends to cause harm, please don't let them off the hook that easily. People need to understand the severity of their actions and how they made you feel. Sometimes, an apology isn't enough. If someone has done something like that to you, they're more than likely going to do it again because they clearly see nothing wrong with their behavior. The person who wronged you must understand that you are not one to fuck with.

Their bad intentions *plus* you're never forgetting them *equals* a better life for you. You don't want to go through the same pain twice.

Second chances are only good if the person has actually changed, or is actively working on avoiding the behavior. For example, I know Lena only acts wayward when she's drinking. She doesn't drink often, and she's working on her behavior. Plus, I just avoid her and alcohol together, so she never has a "second chance" *per se* to treat me like shit again—I established boundaries.

Think long and hard before giving them a second chance. Maybe they deserve another chance if they are truly sorry and working toward change. If they don't seem to think they did anything wrong, then why would you want them in your life? If someone continues to show you that they cannot be trusted, it might be time to move on. To sum it up, don't be afraid to give people second chances, but if they pull the same shit twice, or it was too big of a boundary the first time around, you have every right to walk away and never look back.

People Will Hurt Us for a Variety of Reasons

Life happens, people are human, mistakes are normal, and pain is part of the package. That about sums up all the reasons, right? We're all going to get hurt. It's an unfortunate but essential part of life. While some people will hurt us on purpose, others will do it unintentionally.

Different types of people might try to intentionally hurt us. The first type is what I like to call "the takers." These people only care about themselves and will do whatever it takes to get what they want, even if it means hurting other people. They're manipulative, self-centered, and often have a lot of unresolved issues. The second type of person is what I call "the haters." This group of people gets off on hurting others because someone else is doing better than they are. They're envious and often negative.

The third type of person is what I call "the bullies." These people get their kicks by making other people feel small and powerless. They're insecure, afraid of being exposed, and will do anything to make themselves feel better. No matter what type of person is causing us pain, it's important to remember that we don't have to take it. We can stand up for ourselves, and we can put an end to the cycle of pain.

Some people may hurt you by accident simply because they're stupid or aren't self-aware. Others hurt people because they don't know how to express love properly and act like "silly puppies." They act without thinking and are not emotionally intelligent enough.

A natural response when you get hurt is to speak of revenge. When someone hurts us, we want to hurt them back, or vice versa. It's an eye for an eye. We want them to suffer. They should regret what they've done and see what they've lost. However, revenge only creates more pain and suffering. You should stand your ground, though, and make sure that people understand that it's not beneficial for them to hurt you. Their actions come with consequences. However, this is not applicable if you were hurt by a dumb puppy who knew no better. It's inhumane and pointless to seek revenge because it wasn't intentional.

Associating with people like that is not worth it because they are on such a different level—a level that is way below your own personal development. It would be the same as stabbing an innocent puppy. So, in this case, if you really care about that person, you can try to help them grow if they are looking for help or reevaluate your stance on that person.

If they're unwilling, then let it go, even if it feels impossible or like it will hurt more. The pain we feel from being hurt can be so overwhelming and intense that it feels like it's consuming us. But pain is only temporary. Eventually, it goes away, even if it takes a long time. We can't let the pain define who we are. We are so much more than the hurt we feel.

Be Reasonable and a Fair Bitch

The most important takeaway is to be reasonable and fair. We only engage when someone is pushing us. Otherwise, it's not worth our time or energy. We don't attack others just for fun, nor do we take part in drama for the sake of it. Life's too short to care about what others think or do, especially when they're not worth our time. So, don't be a hater; be NUMB to the haters instead.

We should only fight when people are trying to push us around or waste our time. If this isn't the case, then it's simply not worth it to us. We shouldn't care. Remember, no one gives a fuck about you—so why should you care about them? It's a waste of time, energy, and mental stability. Who the fuck are they to waste our time and energy, and who are we to put that same energy back into them—adding to the vicious cycle of poor behavior? No one is worth that.

Break the cycle of caring what others think or do and be apathetic to the haters. It's not worth our time, nor should we give them satisfaction. Life is too short to be caught up in other people's bullshit, so just be numb to it instead. Screw anyone who tries to bother us for no reason!

Instead of Evening Prayers

1. Analysis at work: Think about a situation when you gave people a second chance. Did you have someone in your life who cherished the second chance and never repeated their mistake? How about people who blew it? What conclusions can you make here?

10

— ⁙ —

DREAM WORKER

You've probably heard that if you work hard enough, you can achieve anything you want in life. While there's no denying that hard work is important, it's not the only factor that determines whether or not you'll be successful. Let's get it straight. You are not fucking special. Forget all those books that told you that you were exceptionally special. Just think about it. Millions of people are reading those books. Everyone thinks they are special.

Hello? We don't live in a utopia—it's the real world! You and I are ordinary people unless you are a genius, which means we fall into a category that includes only 1% of the human population. So, we are all (give or take) alike. Yes, some people are smarter, some people are physically stronger, and some people have more experience, but we have similar dreams, goals, and fears.

What can make you different from the rest of the population is being close to the ground, thinking clearly, and acting fast. Be realistic but also smart and creative. Most of the successful people you know are not better than you. They were just consistent with working on their goals and doing something different from the rest. So, if you want to achieve your goals, you have to work, get creative, and believe in yourself and what you do.

Goals

What are they really? Just a far-off dream? A pipe dream? Something that's so out of reach that you can't even imagine ever achieving it? No. They might seem that way because goals are hard. However, they're supposed to take blood, sweat, and tears. You're not supposed to just wake up one day and achieve them—it takes graft, dedication, and a lot of tenacity.

When it comes to goals, understand that you are not an inspired butterfly who believes in itself and will achieve everything you want just because you say so. No! You are a fucking warrior—a warrior who has to eat ground, burn bridges, and destroy walls if needed. Some goals can be achieved more easily than others. If that's the case, amazing! Always find a shortcut if there is one without affecting the result. However, do what it takes to get everything your way. Do you want something? Go out and get it. It won't be easy, but it will be worth it.

Turn Jealousy Into Motivation

Jealousy is a powerful emotion. Some think it's ugly and destructive. However, jealousy can be a powerful motivator. It's a normal emotion, and people who say they don't get jealous are liars. If you see someone achieving the goal you want, don't be jealous of them; be motivated by them. Use it as fuel for your rocket engine.

Use their success to show you what's possible and to push you to achieve your own dreams. Jealousy is a wasted emotion if you allow it to consume you. It will only lead to problems. However, if you use it as motivation, it can be a powerful tool to help you achieve your goals. Let their success power you up to act on your pursuits.

Be a Bulldozer

Be like a bulldozer—nothing can stop you. When people see you're determined to accomplish your dream, they'll get out of your way. If you come in like a wrecking ball and plow through everything, people will eventually get out of your way. When people notice you're passionate about something and won't give up, they'll support you. They will see you differently, and eventually, they'll treat you differently. Just keep going and let nothing stop you.

Don't Lower Your Bar

"The sky's the limit," is what they say, and it's true. Life and goals don't come with limits. They may be difficult, which may make you want to give up, but your abilities are limitless. Don't ever lower your bar or settle for less. Keep hustling and pushing yourself forward.

If you reach your milestone, fantastic! Keep your standards high, though. Don't take one step forward and two steps back. Continue to focus on your progress—create a new, bigger, and bolder goal to accomplish.

If you have not reached your goal yet, don't worry. Just keep moving forward and reach for the stars because they will not fall into your lap—you need to go out and get them. So, if you're feeling stuck, remember this: Don't lower your bar; raise your game.

Never Work for Free

In a world where everyone is trying to get ahead, being strategic about the opportunities you take on is critical. You don't want to be taken advantage of, and you don't want to end up working for free. Sometimes we're too nice for our own good, and we do a job or a favor for free when we shouldn't. However, labor should be paid for. You should always get paid for your work—one way or another.

It doesn't matter what you do or who your client is—you should never work for free. If you're a photographer, don't let your friends take advantage of you by asking you to shoot their weddings for free. If you're a tattoo artist, don't let your family members or friends get away with not paying you for the art you created on them. Your time and labor are valuable, so always make sure you're getting compensated fairly.

Of course, there are exceptions to this rule—but there is a time and a place for it. Once you've established yourself, make sure you're getting paid what you're worth, and let no one take advantage of you or your talents. Be mindful of the situation and make sure you're being fairly compensated for your time and labor.

Visualization

Visualization is a great tool. It is the act of creating a mental image of what you want to achieve. You can use it to see yourself where you want to be. It will help you stay excited and get in motion. In fact, some of the most successful people in the world are also the ones who have learned to harness the power of visualization. When you visualize your goals, you are essentially planting the seeds of your success in your mind, and like any excellent gardener knows, the better you take care of those seeds, the more likely they are to grow into beautiful, bountiful plants.

So, what does that mean for you? It means that if you want to achieve something, you need to see yourself achieving it. You need to believe that it is possible. Only then will you be able to take steps to make it happen. Plenty of visualization techniques and tools exist to help. Everyone can find a few that suit them, and there is an ocean of information available on the internet, which is why we will not dive deep into the tools here.

However, don't expect to visualize your success and then sit on your ass. Your dreams don't come without you working for them. You may come close to some goals, but you still have to get up and be in great shape to get what you want.

Work on your goals and visualize the final results. *Work and visualize.*

The bottom line is this: If you want something, work for it. It won't be easy, but it will be worth it. You can achieve anything you set your mind to..

When I was a young boy, I wanted to be a famous singer and dreamed of being on TV; I loved singing. In my teen years, I started writing songs. When I was 18, I moved to Moscow and wrote a bangin' pop song. When I first sent it to record labels, they ignored me, so I changed my tactics. I created a fake email address, impersonating some young woman. Then, I sent emails to the management of all the record labels in the city. The email said something like: "Hey guys, I'm a huge music lover, and I know about your label because I'm a fan of one of your artists. I came across a young talent recently (see the song attached). Why are you not working with him?"

I purposely didn't attach any contact info for "the young talent," otherwise, it would look obvious. Nobody responded to the email, although I didn't really expect them to. I was sure they had read it, which was enough for me. On top of that, I also asked all my friends to call the biggest radio stations and ask for my song. When radio associates couldn't find the song in the library, my friends would say something like, "Weird. It's a new artist from [label]. Are you sure you can't play the song?"

A few weeks later, I received a message from the A&R manager of one of the world's largest record labels. According to the manager, they recently discovered my song and would love to have a meeting. That's how I got my first music video, got into Russia's MTV Top 10, and was heavily rotated on local radio stations.

In the long run, it didn't work out, mostly because I became lazy and lost interest. The way I pictured show business wasn't accurate in real life, but I got my 15 minutes of fame. I made my childhood dream come true. I was on TV and radio, was invited to interviews, and got to sing my ass off.

As I did, you should find your own way to move forward with your goals. You can't sit around waiting for your goals to just happen. You are responsible for doing the work. You need to hustle.

My dreams and goals are different today. I wouldn't want to be famous even if I received a lot of money. However, if you want something bad enough, put in the work and be creative. Get out there and make it happen. Do everything in your power—remember, don't take "no" for an answer.

Feed Yourself With Related Imagery

Can you picture a color you've never seen? How about an animal you've never seen? The brain thinks in images, and what you envision in your mind is a combination of some things you are familiar with. So, what does this have to do with achieving your dreams? It means that if you want to create something new or achieve something great, you need to feed yourself with related imagery. For instance, if you want to be a brilliant writer, read as much as you can. Bask in writing tools and other writers' companies.

If you want to be a great artist, fill your life with as much art as possible. Go to museums and art shows. Play with paint, crayons, and markers—everything and anything that can spark that creativity. Consume everything that has to do with art. If you want to start your own business, surround yourself with successful entrepreneurs and resources that can help you achieve your dream.

If you want to achieve something great, you need to surround yourself with related items. The more related imagery you feed your brain, the easier it will be for you to create something new and original. So, if you want to achieve something great, make sure you surround yourself with items related to your goals.

Creative numbness can be awakened with inspiration. Sometimes the best ideas come from the most unlikely sources, so don't be afraid to explore and experiment. The more you try new challenges, the more likely you are to find an activity that inspires you.

Track Your Progress

One of the best pieces of advice I've ever heard is to track your progress. Sometimes, without visual representation, it's easy to feel like you're not making any headway, especially when pursuing long-term goals. However, if you take the time to track your progress, you can see just how far you've come and how much closer you are to your goals. This will keep you motivated and focused on the prize.

For instance, let's say you've decided to lose weight and work out more. However, you didn't weigh or measure yourself before you started a workout plan. Nor did you take progress pictures. So, after working out for two months, you feel like you have made no progress, and are tempted to give up.

Now, what if someone showed you a picture from two months ago that you took with a group of friends? You might look at that person and think, "Wow, I looked different then. I can't believe I've come so far." This is the power of tracking your progress. It allows you to see just how far you've come and how much closer you are to your goals.

You should track your progress in whatever way works best for you. Going back to the weight loss examples, if you had been tracking your progress, you would have seen that you actually lost 20 pounds and gained muscle mass. You would have seen the hard work you put in paying off immediately, instead of looking back at an old picture when you feel discouraged. This would have kept you motivated to keep going. So, whatever goals you're pursuing, be sure to track your progress. This will help you stay focused and motivated.

Journal or Write Regularly

Writing is a great way to track your progress. In fact, if imposter syndrome is a concern for you, writing about your journey can help you find clarity. This can be a blog, a journal, a spreadsheet, or even just some regular posts on social media. Your journey will be more fun and enjoyable when you track your progress in some way.

Journaling helps with imposter syndrome, as I mentioned earlier. Imposter syndrome is when you feel like you're not good enough or that you don't deserve your success, which is a common feeling among entrepreneurs, artists, and other professionals. However, everyone feels that way at some point. The key is to push through the feelings and continue working toward your goals. Then, you'll see the work you've put in and the correlation between the effort and the success.

Sharing Goals With Others

Aside from tracking your goals personally, you can share them with others. This type of accountability can prompt you to stay on track and motivated. Some people don't like to share their goals or progress and prefer to "move in silence." The route you choose is completely up to you, and one is not really "better" than the other.

Some people truly believe that if they tell others about their dreams or goals, they will never come true. They think that by talking about their goals, they are jinxing themselves. In my opinion, this isn't the case. If you don't want to tell anyone, then don't, but don't be afraid to share. It's about perspective—do you not want to tell them because you don't want them to overshadow your efforts or talk you out of it? Or because you don't want to be jinxed?

As I said earlier, visualization works and can work really well. However, it can also work both ways—meaning negatively and positively. The visualization only sees the main idea. This tool doesn't focus on verb phrases. For example, let's say you visualize "to be healthy." The universe only hears "healthy." It doesn't hear the "to be" part. This means you will attract health.

However, let's say you rephrase it to "I never want to be sick." Well then, the universe will hear "sick." Here's another example: Let's say you tell a group of people that you want to become a doctor. Some salty as fuck people may say, "Oh, [insert your name] will never become a doctor," or "I hope [insert your name] will never be a doctor." However, although these are negative statements about you and your goals, the universe only hears "doctor" along with your name. I see it as a benefit because all those people will help you make your visualization statement stronger for the universe to hear. Now, instead of just you visualizing yourself as a doctor, a bunch of others do the same. Thanks, besties.

In my opinion, this suggests that it's not just visualizing your goals that's important, but the number of people you share your dream with. The more people you tell, the more likely it is to come true.

You will also create a certain mental image of yourself for others. If you say you want to be a doctor, they're going to picture you in scrubs with a stethoscope around your neck. This is what we call a "self-fulfilling prophecy." It helps to create a new reality about yourself.

Additionally, if you share your ideas and goals with others, they may help you. By talking about what you want to achieve, you may realize that some of your goals are actually achievable. Other people may give you resources or advice on how to achieve what you want in a more efficient way.

Sharing your goals with others also allows you to be held accountable. If someone knows that you're trying to achieve a particular goal, they can help you stay on track. They can encourage you when you're feeling down and motivate you to keep going.

Stay Consistent

Consistency is the key to success. You need to be consistent with your actions if you want to achieve your goals. This doesn't mean you have to perform the same actions every day. It just means that you need to be consistently working toward your goals.

You can achieve anything you set your mind to. Just remember to keep your mind focused on what you want to achieve and let nothing stop you. Some days, you will have more energy and motivation than others. That's normal. Just don't let those days be an excuse to slack off. The most successful people in the world are usually the ones who are most consistent with their actions. They show up every day and do the work even when they don't feel like it.

Every time you get discouraged, remind yourself of who you are and be that person. It's kind of like "fake it 'til you make it," but not exactly. If you just started working toward a new profession, for example, don't wait for that imposter syndrome to disappear. Don't wait for 10 years of experience to finally validate yourself. As soon as you decide to become someone, you are already that someone. Keep reminding yourself that you are changing and think like the person you're becoming. Develop the mindset of someone who is already in the position you want to be in.

When I switched careers and started learning software development, I would often get discouraged. I would look at other people who had been coding for years and think to myself, *I'll never be as good as them.* My brain would tell me, *This is too difficult. I'm way too dumb for this. I can't do it.* Then I realized everyone starts somewhere, and the only way to get better is to keep practicing.

So, every time I noticed that negative self-talk, I would tell myself, *I'm a fucking software engineer! I know how to solve problems. I'm good at it, and there is no way I'm going to fail to succeed.* I just kept showing up every day and doing the work, and eventually, I got to where I wanted to be.

Success takes time, so be patient. The journey is just as important as the destination. You will make mistakes along the way, but that's okay. It's all part of the learning process. Just don't give up on your dreams. Pursue them with passion and consistency, and you will achieve them. Surround yourself with imagery and items related to your goals, be motivated by those who are already successful, and stay consistent with your efforts. These are the keys to success.

Hire a Professional

When it comes to your dreams and goals, you need to be smart about the decisions you make. Sometimes, it's worth it to hire a professional to outsource some tasks. Yes, we have bills to pay, but your time is more costly than the service. Find a business consultant if you want to start your own business. Consult with a personal trainer if you want to get in shape.

Investing in professionals will help you save time, money, and energy in the long run. Hiring a professional is an investment, but one that will pay off. Be smart about the decisions you make and the people you surround yourself with. If you're serious about achieving your dreams, don't be afraid to invest in yourself.

Save your time and pay for a professional. You don't need to learn every single subject or talent on the planet. You want to focus on your goals and not get sidetracked. When you're trying to accomplish a task, make sure you have the right team in place to help you succeed. You can't do it all alone, so don't be afraid to ask for help.

Utilize the tools available and concentrate on something you do best. You can use a million different ways to crack an egg, but you only need to find the one that benefits you the most. When it comes to your dreams and goals, focus on your strengths. Outsource the rest of the tasks to others, as much as possible. There's no shame in admitting that you need help. In fact, it's a sign of strength. Asking for help shows you're willing to invest in yourself and your dreams.

For instance, if you're training for a marathon and need some help with your diet and exercise plan, hiring a personal trainer may be the best way to help you reach your goal. Many professionals are available to help you achieve your goals. All you need to do is to invest in yourself and ask for help.

If You're Paying, You're the Boss

Sometimes we're too worried about being pushy or demanding—even if we're the ones paying for the service. If you're paying for a service, you're the boss. You have the right to ask for the service you were promised and expect to get it. For instance, if you hire a personal trainer and they're not delivering what was discussed or are doing poorly, speak up. It's your money, time, and energy, so don't be afraid to demand what you deserve. The same goes for any service you're paying for.

If you're not happy with the results, then demand better. Remember, you're the boss—you have a right to expect the best for your money. Don't be a pushover; make sure you're getting what you paid for. You don't have to be an ignorant or arrogant boss. However, if you paid for something, demand the service and quality you were promised. If they cannot deliver as promised, then change the provider.

Don't Listen to Everybody and Don't Take Advice From Non-Experts

One of the worst things you can do for yourself is to take advice from people who don't know what they're talking about. Unfortunately, many people do this. They listen to their friends or family members, who do not know what they're talking about. Then they take this unwelcome, terrible advice and run with it, which leads them astray.

You should only take advice from people who are experts in the field you're interested in. If you're trying to be healthier, don't take advice from your friend who is not in the best shape. Take advice from a nutritionist or dietician. If you're trying to start a business, don't take advice from your unemployed friend. Take advice from someone who is already successful in business. You get the idea. Don't listen to everybody and only take advice from experts.

Timing

Time flies, and we are only moving in one direction. Some people attach their age to their goals and limit themselves. However, goals have no age restrictions. It doesn't matter how old you are—you can always reach brilliant milestones. Some people become billionaires at age 21, and others start their first business at 70.

We all have our own schedules, and everyone is born with a unique set of advantages and disadvantages. You are already on that train going toward success; you are just on a different route or schedule. You only need to make sure you get the most out of it and that the train conductor doesn't kick you off.

Some of the most successful people in the world started later in life. J.K. Rowling was rejected by dozens of publishers before finally getting published at age 32. Colonel Sanders didn't start selling Kentucky Fried Chicken until he was 65. The list goes on and on.

Some people have to run barefoot to hop onto the success train while learning how to run at the same time. Some people get a head start by having their parents buy them the fanciest pair of shoes and a golden ticket. Don't be sad if someone is more privileged. Don't give up on your dreams because you think you're getting too old or because people tell you it's too late.

It's never too late to do something great. Results take time. Think about Samuel L. Jackson; he didn't make it big until his mid-40s. Take your time to train, learn, and overtake. If you have more advantages than others, acknowledge them and use them to your full potential. Be grateful for your advantages, and don't waste your gifts. Be proud, but never arrogant.

When I was 17, I attended the college I spoke about earlier, and I barely had money. To make ends meet, I would do homework, labs, and presentations for my classmates for extra cash. The income I made went straight to food and rent. Since I didn't have my own computer, I would spend hours in the town library after school.

One evening, I stopped by my friend's house. We were sitting in the living room when one of their friends, whom I had never met, arrived. He took his shoes off when he started laughing and shouting, "Who wears these ugly-ass shoes? I wouldn't even wear them to walk on horse shit because it would be disrespectful to the horse!" Guess whose shoes he was talking about?

They were my shoes. He was right. My shoes were ugly as fuck. They also weren't warm enough for brutal Russian winters, and I had to wear three to four pairs of socks to make it bearable. I felt extremely embarrassed. Looking back, I know I probably shouldn't have felt that way, but I was young and dependent on social acceptance.

Thankfully, the shoe conversation went no further, and everyone let it go. However, going back to the guy who made fun of my shoes, he was from a middle-class family and had a relatively good life compared to others. Since that day, we have moved through life at different speeds with distinct ambitions and goals. We had different variables at the beginning of the adulthood road, but I overtook his level of success tremendously.

My life is eventful, and I'm skilled. My net worth is more significant than his, and I'm not bragging. I never tried to make him feel any worse about himself, and I'm not trying to do that to you. It's an example of how you can overshadow the privileged—that most of the time, we are way behind others, but that doesn't mean you have to feel discouraged. You can always catch up and overtake them if you wish. You can bypass them on their route. They might be on the train, but maybe you can take a plane. It's your choice to either complain about everything and everyone for your state of life or take responsibility for yourself and answer to yourself.

Life Is Not a Race

Racing can be fun but also exhausting. Don't forget, life is a voyage to be experienced. Take your time. Appreciate the process and the journey. If you want to get somewhere, you will get there—do not forget to enjoy life along the way.

It's okay to slow down. You can take a break. It's even okay to stop and get on a different train. You can go from slow to fast, fast to slow or stay in neutral. Life isn't a race. As long as you are alive, there is always time to start over. Do not compare your life to anyone else's. You do not know what their journey is about or what they have been through. Someone else being ahead of you doesn't mean you are behind. Being in front of someone else doesn't mean you are ahead. You are on your own journey. Just focus on your destination. Focus on your life. You need to make sure you're enjoying the life you're living—you don't want to get burned out.

For example, for a long time, I had a powerful belief that I would be a terrible driver. I didn't know how to drive, and I lacked confidence. I often envisioned myself wreaking havoc the moment I hit the road. When I was 17, I was trying to learn how to drive in Russia. When I look back, I realize that the instructor was a fucking moron. He taught me stick shift and was rude. He would scream at me and call me names, which I think caused my lack of driving confidence. After my terrible experience, I gave up on driving.

Since I was living in Moscow, I didn't really need a car. Then, when I came to the United States, I lived in New York City, where a car still wasn't necessary. I was doing perfectly fine until I moved to Florida. Life forced me to give driving another shot. So, I hired an instructor, learned the basics, and passed my driving test. Even after that, though, I was still terrified of driving. However, the need for me to drive was stronger than my fears. Every day, I forced myself to drive somewhere. I tried to get as much time on the road as I could to get as comfortable as possible with the driving process.

A few weeks later, my anxieties were better, but I still had some insecurities, which led me to the crazy idea of taking a road trip to visit every state. At the time, the crazy thought made me laugh. I struggled to drive back and forth from the coffee shop—how was I going to drive across the continental US? However, then my mindset changed from *why in the world would I do that?* to *why the fuck not?* I could explore all the places I have always wanted to visit and get the driving experience.

For a year, that's exactly what I did. I drove around the country. I worked remotely and drove on many roads—deserted, icy, mountainous, country, coastal, steep, and so on. During that trip, I put 55,000 miles on my car. I got the driving experience I was missing in my life, and let me tell you, I am an amazing driver. I'm a defensive, responsible driver, and I love it. In fact,

I wish I had done it sooner, but as I said, we all have our own speed. Our comfortability. For me, 28 years old was the right age to learn to drive. For most, it's 16, but who cares? What does it matter?

Lost? Develop a Plan

Ok, life is a journey, but how good is your sense of direction? If you feel like you are lost, it is time to develop a plan. This will help you focus on your goals and give you a sense of direction. Think about what you want to achieve in life and write it down. Develop a roadmap that will help get you there, and then enjoy the ride. Changes may occur along the way. There will be detours, roadblocks, and delays. You may even have to go back and forth a few times before you reach your destination. However, if you keep your eye on the prize, you will eventually get there.

Think of life as a road trip across the United States. You would never just get in the car and start driving without a map or plan. You need to know where you're going, where you're going to visit, how you're going to get there, and what to do when you do arrive. The same is true for life. You need to know where you want to go and what you want to do before you can hit the road to success. So, take some time, develop a plan, and enjoy the journey. Life is an adventure, so make sure you're prepared for the ride.

If you're afraid you won't be good at something, just throw yourself at it anyway. Just do it. Consider the rule of 10,000 hours of work. You can be good at anything if you just put in 10,000 hours of intensive practice to master complex skills. As Malcolm Gladwell believed, you don't have to practice for precisely 10,000 hours, but the more time you spend on a task, the greater your proficiency. Put your time into actually mastering the task—how many hours away are you?

Instead of Evening Prayers

1. What is your primary goal? Where are you headed long-term?

2. Write a brief paragraph to describe how the completed quest looks and feels in your mind. What is the vision you're working toward?

3. Break your goal into smaller chunks. Create a plan. Label each phase, its requirements, and set a deadline for each. It's vital to have a schedule and keep yourself in a rhythm.

4. Think and list qualifications, resources, and tools you already have to help achieve it. What obstacles exist at the moment? Create a plan on how to eliminate them. For example, if you have time management issues, get educated on that topic.

5. Think about people you know who can help you at every stage of your journey. Schedule a meeting with them. Ask for help. It can be knowledge support, financial assistance, network sharing, etc.

6. Are there some routine side tasks that you can outsource? If so, do it.

7. Commit to a routine to work on your goal consistently, even if it's 15 minutes a day. Say an affirmation, visualize your goal, or research your project.

8. Journal everything you do. Put together the plan, deadlines, people you've spoken to, and

your progress. Create and follow the roadmap right in front of you always.

11

— • —

401-ME

You are an asset. Think of yourself as the entire stock market. Your hair, your skin, your nails, your body, your brain, and your soul—these are all stocks. You need to invest in them all in order to get the best return. The more you invest in yourself, the higher your returns will be. There are many people who think that they can cut corners in their personal care and still come out ahead. They try to save money by using cheap products or by skipping steps in their daily routines.

This is a mistake. When you cut corners on your personal care, development, education, or pleasures, you are really just cheating yourself, and the quality of your life will suffer. You are the only asset in your life that you can be 100% sure about. You will always get a return on such an investment. So, make sure that you invest in yourself wisely—you should be your biggest asset in your portfolio. Choose quality over quantity every time.

One day, I was searching for online courses, and I came across one that seemed interesting. However, I was weary because I wasn't sure if the course would present enough new information for me. I confided in a friend, who told me a simple phrase that has stuck in my mind ever since. She told me, "Even if you learn one new thing, your investment is worth it." This phrase has helped me a lot throughout my life. It's not about the quantity, it's about the benefits in general.

Treat all your investments in yourself like that. It's not about how much you will get out of it. It's about getting something—anything—out of it. As long as you are growing, you are not losing. Some investments bring us a triple return. Others bring us 10 times or 10,000 times the return, just like the stock market. However, even if an investment only gives you a single return, it is still worth it.

Don't Be Cheap

Money makes the world go round, or so they say. While it may not be the most important aspect of life, it is still a crucial part of it. One way to be wise with your money is to invest it in yourself. That's right—invest in yourself in every way.

Never try to compromise the quality. Don't be a cheapskate toward yourself. Spend money and time on yourself. Get a massage, go to the spa, get your hair done, buy new clothes—do whatever makes you feel good. Don't forget to invest in your health as well. Go to the doctor, get regular checkups, and take care of yourself. The better you feel, the better your life will be. Investing in yourself covers many aspects of your life—education, mental and physical health, financial stability, and pleasures. Every dollar you spend on yourself will provide great returns.

Remember, you need to be in tip-top shape to fully enjoy life. If you haven't helped yourself, you can't help others. You can't reach success if you haven't put in the work. You won't be happy if you're not content.

Here's something to ponder on: Your mattress. The average human spends about a third of their life sleeping, meaning if you have a mattress that's 10 years old, you've already slept on it for about three years. Most people change their mattresses every 7–10 years (Foley, 2020). We spend a lot of time on an object that is constantly being used, and by the time we're ready to get rid of it, it's usually because it's lost its shape or it isn't as comfortable as it once was.

Yet, most people don't spend nearly enough money on their mattresses. They'll go out and spend $1,000 on a new TV, but with their bed, they'll try to get by with the cheapest one they can find. Why? This is a mistake because a good mattress is an investment that will pay off in the long run.

It will last you for many years, and it will make an enormous difference in the quality of your sleep. In fact, studies have shown that a good mattress can actually improve your health (Jacobson et al., 2009). We don't only do this with mattresses but with everything in our lives. We try to save money in all the wrong places, and it ends up costing us in the long run.

One day, I was at the gym, and a man approached me. I have a few tattoos, and on my calf, I have a cat-stranaut (a.k.a. a space kitty), as some people call it. He asked me how old the tattoo was, and at the time it was about two years old. His eyebrows rose in disbelief. He showed me his shoulder tattoo and asked me to guess how old that tattoo was. To me, the tattoo looked about 15 to 20 years old, but I didn't want to sound rude, so I undershot and told him eight.

He laughed—the tattoo was three months old. I couldn't believe him. It was my turn to be shocked. He told me he learned the lessons of life the hard way. He didn't want to spend a lot of money, but he wanted a tattoo. So, he went to the cheapest tattoo artist in town. I was surprised because, to me, this was an obvious lesson, but apparently not to him.

Now, don't get me wrong. Cheap service doesn't always equate to terrible service, and expensive service doesn't mean it will be excellent. However, price should be one of the smaller factors in your decision. You should first consider the quality of the service, your comfort levels, the end results, and your experience. Take all of those aspects together and then consider the price. Is what you're getting worth the bang for the buck?

Don't be afraid to spend money on yourself and your well-being. You can save cash on a Christmas gift for your annoying-ass aunt, but never try to cut corners for yourself.

People try to save money on dentists, education, travel packages, and even boob jobs. Then they wonder why their titties are lopsided, why their veneers are falling out, or why the experience was simply unsatisfactory. They tried to save money and got what they paid for—cheap service. If you want something done right, pay for proper service. *You get what you pay for* is an old saying but it is especially true with investing in yourself. If you want something of quality, then pay for it.

Saving Money on Yourself Is a Gamble

Let's say you head out to Vegas or Atlantic City for the weekend. You're feeling lucky and decide to hit up the casino. You walk around looking for a cheap table with a $5 or $10 minimum. After finding one, you pull up a seat, and after an hour or so, you're down $100. You're not too worried because you budgeted $500 in gambling money for the weekend, so you find another cheap table and pull up a seat. A few hours later, you're down $300. Now you're getting worried.

You can't seem to win at any of the cheap tables, so you decide to sit at a $25 minimum table. Do you see how, as you lost, you spent more? Then, at the end, you pay more per bet in order to win your money back. It's called chasing your losses, and the same is true with investing in yourself. When you try to save money, you're gambling with your future, with your well-being.

You get a cheap massage, and it's not excellent. Maybe it's too hard, too soft, or the massage therapist wasn't just good. Now you're out $60 and have not had a positive experience, which means you still have to find someone to give you a decent massage. You could have just spent $120 on a great massage in the first place and been done with it. It would have been worth it because you would have walked out feeling relaxed and rejuvenated instead of stressed and angry. Now you paid the $60 for the first massage and will probably end up shelling out another $120, anyway.

When you are trying to save money on yourself, you're basically gambling. You can get lucky, but you also might not. The question is, how comfortable are you with gambling with your own being?

Saving money and investing in yourself apply not only to pleasures or appearance, they can also concern your education and knowledge. Some people may not want to go back to school or take an online course because of the money or time involved. However, remember what my friend said—as long as you learn one new thing, your time and money were spent wisely.

Your education, personal growth, and knowledge are not qualities that you can take for granted. Work on them in order to be successful, both personally and financially. If you want to know something, ask a friend or someone who knows. Find out what books or websites offer useful information about the subject. Or else, continue searching for them online, where numerous resources are available. As the old saying goes, *Nothing ventured, nothing gained.* So, don't be afraid to try new things. Expand your mind and knowledge by learning something new today—like the information in this book.

Aging Well

They say that age is just a number, but when you look in the mirror, you see the effects of time on your face. You might feel insecure, unattractive, and even depressed. However, have you seen a well-aged person? You know, like the 75-year-old grandpa who still has a tight ass and can outrun you? Or the 80-year-old woman that looks like she's in her 50s? Have you spoken to them about how they preserved a healthy and happy appearance?

What do they have in common? They've invested in themselves constantly. They ate healthy food, engaged in healthy habits, and participated in sports. Their mental health was a priority, and they went for annual checkups. As we age, we need to make ourselves feel good about ourselves and our appearance. If we don't, we'll age before our time. Some people are naturally blessed with good genes. They might not have to do as much to look their best. For the rest of us, we have to work harder or invest more, but it's worth it when we see the results.

Wrinkles

When speaking to older people, have you noticed how some of them provide a warm, friendly, and happy vibe while others appear grumpy and unapproachable? Do you know why? It's their wrinkles—their wrinkles give them away. For example, some wrinkles from happiness or laughing, such as those around the eye line and cheeks.

Other wrinkles are from stress, unhappiness, and anger, like the *frown* wrinkle, the vertical wrinkle between the eyebrows. I personally want to give off a happy vibe when I'm old, so I invest in myself now. The investment return affects not only the quality of your life but also your appearance. So, when you're budgeting for your future, don't forget to include money for investments in yourself. It may seem like a lot now, but it will be worth it in the long run.

Don't Treat Yourself to Unhealthy Desires

After a long week of work, treating yourself with unhealthy rewards like excessive drinking, binge eating, or smoking is tempting. However, these unhealthy coping mechanisms will only make you feel worse in the long run. Not only will you have to deal with the hangover or the calories, but you'll also have to deal with the guilt and shame of giving in to your unhealthy desires.

For instance, I have some friends who think the best way to unwind on a Friday night is to go bar hopping and get wasted, but what they don't realize is that they're just setting themselves up for a weekend of recovery. They wake up feeling groggy and dehydrated. Then they spend the rest of the time nursing their hangovers. By the time Sunday night rolls around, they're already dreading Monday morning. Instead of starting their week off on a positive note, they're already feeling stressed and fatigued. They end up exhausting their bodies even more instead of prompting the hard-earned recovery they crave.

While there's nothing wrong with blowing off steam with a few drinks (in moderation, of course), some people often forget the more healthy ways to alleviate stress. They could engage in many activities that don't result in hangovers or regretful eating choices.

For example, they could take a relaxing bath, go for a massage, or spend time outdoors in nature.

Relaxation and rejuvenation are crucial for living a healthy life, both physically and mentally. When we don't take care of ourselves, it shows in our appearance. We look tired, haggard, and stressed. To avoid this, include some "me time" in your schedule to relax and rejuvenate. It doesn't have to be anything fancy; just do something that makes you feel good. It could be as simple as reading a book, taking a yoga class, or getting a manicure.

Your physical and mental health go hand in hand. This means eating healthy foods, exercising regularly, and getting enough sleep. These activities will help you unwind without harming your body in the process. Incorporate a variety of rewards, and don't harm yourself with unhealthy habits.

Instead of Evening Prayers

1. When was the last time you invested in your-

self? Set aside a portion of your income toward a personal investment.

2. Differentiate that investment portfolio by adding the most important asset—yourself. How can you invest in yourself?

3. Can you recall times when you wanted to save money but were unsatisfied with the result? What did you learn from it?

4. Think about three things you could spend your money on to spike the value of your self-investment.

12

— · —

BUSY BEE

"You're a busy little bee, aren't you?" My friends and family would say that to me all the time, and I used to think it was a bit of an insult as if it were wrong for me to want to be busy and productive and as if I should lie down and relax as others told me to. But now I realize that being busy is a good thing. It means that you're productive and that you're making the most of your time, which is important because time is precious.

Time is the one commodity we can never get back. When we're busy, we can finish more achievements in a day and more goals in a lifetime. However, it's not just about being busy for the sake of being busy. There's an art to being busy, which starts with inspiration and planning. You're more likely to be productive when you have a plan for your day. You're less likely to get sidetracked or waste time, which is crucial because every minute counts. Every minute should be filled with moments that inspire, motivate, or spark you to be your best self.

The Power Behind "Awe"

Awe is a powerful and inspiring emotion. It can slow down time and make us feel more present in the moment. When we experience awe, our focus expands. We become more aware of our surroundings and connect to something larger than ourselves. Awe is a feeling that can be inspired by nature, art, music, or even a simple act of kindness. When we experience it, our lives become richer and more meaningful.

Awe is often described as a feeling of reverence or admiration, but it's much more than that. Awe is a complex emotion that includes elements of fear, wonder, and joy. It's an emotion that can be both exhilarating and overwhelming. Awe is also a powerful motivator. Studies have shown that awe can inspire us to be more generous, more curious, and more likely to help others. Awe can also make us feel more connected to the world.

Stop for a moment and think about a scene, person, or activity that fills you with awe. Maybe it's the vastness of the night sky or the beauty of a snowflake. Maybe it's the laughter of a child or the love of a family member. Experience the smell, sound, and feel of the moment. Let the feeling of awe wash over you. Awe is a powerful emotion that can profoundly impact our lives.

In Chapter 10, I shared the story of my road trip when I was traveling across the country. I hopped from state to state and from national park to national park. The scenery changed nonstop. I was filled with new experiences, beautiful nature, and unique people. A week would feel like a month. When you live an eventful, busy life—not repetitive, but diversely busy—you notice that time seems to slow down.

Your brain becomes more efficient at handling all the new information and experiences. You will feel more present in each moment. Enhance your life with events. Diversify your routine. Try new activities. You don't need to travel the world to do this, though it helps. Just look for opportunities in your day-to-day life to create moments of awe.

Mix and Match

The key to being busy is to mix and match your activities. With a variety of activities at your fingertips, you never get bored, and you have opportunities to learn something new. However, with only so many hours in a day and only so much energy to spend, it's tough to find the right balance. Then you risk burnout. Burnout is when you're so exhausted that you can't function properly, you're irritable, your work suffers, or you become less productive.

The balance between work and play, between engaging in challenging and fun activities, is crucial. To avoid burnout, arranging for some downtime and engaging in an activity you enjoy with no obligations will help.

Your body will let you know when it wants you to slow down or just do nothing. Listen to it. Enjoy your solitude. Sometimes it's fine to just do nothing—to solely recharge and absorb energy. Never feel guilty for doing nothing. For instance, on a cold, rainy day, your body might beg you for a cozy night at home instead of hitting the gym. This might include reading a book, taking a walk, or listening to music. Then, when you're feeling rested and refreshed, you'll be able to tackle your goals with renewed energy and enthusiasm.

Be a Smart Bee

Don't just be a busy bee; be a smart bee—be smart with your business. Plan and organize your time so that you can make the most of every minute. Be productive and spend your time being intentional. Set goals for yourself. Write down what you want to achieve in the short, medium, and long term. Make a plan of action to reach those goals. Then take small steps every day to move closer to them.

Experiment or take a new class. Start a new hobby. Join a club or organization and broaden your social circle. The more you do, the more you'll realize that there's so much to life that you haven't experienced yet. You'll feel a sense of accomplishment and pride as you complete new challenges. You'll also feel more motivated to keep going and do even more.

Being busy is good for you. It keeps your mind active and engaged. You can learn new subjects and grow as a person from it. It gives you a sense of purpose and meaning. Plus, being smart and busy is a vaccine for depression. From my experience, I can tell you that a bored mind is the Devil's workshop. When you're busy, you don't have time to dwell on negative thoughts or worry about situations that you can't control. Instead, you're constantly experiencing life and all that it has to offer.

So, don't be afraid to be busy. Embrace it and enjoy every moment. That way, you'll be more productive, feel better about yourself, and make the most of every day.

Plan Before You Jump

When you're feeling overwhelmed, it can be tempting to just jump into action and start working on whatever is in front of you, but this isn't always the best approach. Spontaneity can be fun, but it's not always the most effective way to get a task done. It's exhausting, and it can lead to burnout.

The key is to find a balance between spontaneity and planning. You don't want to be so rigid that you never try a new activity or take risks. However, you also don't want to be so spontaneous that you're constantly putting out fires and getting nothing done.

The best way to find this balance is to plan before you jump. Keep the spontaneous spirit, but still do some homework and do the planning. Don't overstress about planning your life; keep it simple and structured. When you have a goal that you want to achieve, take some time to think about it. What are your objectives? What are the steps that you need to take to reach your goal? This will give you a roadmap to follow so that you know where you're going and how you're going to get there.

Don't Postpone

Sometimes life can feel like a never-ending to-do list. You have a million things to do and not enough time to do them. So, you keep putting them off, but then the list just gets longer and longer. Your tasks become more daunting.

Don't let this happen to you. Don't postpone your life. If you have something that you want to do, do it now. Don't wait for the perfect time because the perfect time will never come. Your to-do list will always have a million and one tasks. This doesn't apply to just your goals. It applies to your day-to-day tasks too.

Don't procrastinate, especially if it's a simple business. Do it now and get it over with. You'll feel so much better once it's done, and you'll be one step closer to completing your goals. Use David Allen's two-minute rule to help you with this (Allen, n.d.). If it takes less than two minutes, do it now. It's a very simple and extremely useful rule.

So, don't be afraid to be busy. Don't wait to travel the world or start your own business. Do it now and live your life to the fullest.

Nostalgia Is a Swamp

To me, nostalgia is a negative emotion that pretends to be warm and fuzzy. In a particular moment, reminiscing might help, but it can also make you feel terrible. Don't get too caught up in the past or the future. The present is where you should be focusing. Nostalgia is a swamp. It reminds you of what you enjoyed and wished for. However, in the same setup, you will never experience those situations again, so instead, you become sad about those delightful times.

Nostalgia drags us back and tries to keep us in the past. It's not a wonderful emotion. It doesn't make you feel good, and you may feel worse because of it. I always try to avoid it. If it happens, I do my best to limit my time of being nostalgic. We always want to look and move forward. That's the best way to live.

You shouldn't be living in the past or constantly looking forward to the future. You should be focused on the present. That's where the magic happens. That's where you should live your life.

Importance of Meditation

Meditation and new-age medicine are quite popular nowadays, aren't they? I'm not one to judge whether they are "cool" or not, but I will say that they have some benefits that you may not be aware of. When you meditate, you're training your mind to be in the present moment, which, as I mentioned above, is crucial to enjoying your life. You're teaching your mind to focus on one object and let go of the thoughts that float around in it. This skill is extremely useful to have in life. If you can learn to focus on one object while ignoring other distractions, you'll be able to get a lot more done.

You don't have to sit still to meditate. Meditating is a mindful practice, and you can be mindful of your surroundings no matter what you're doing. You can walk, cook, clean, or work and still practice mindfulness. The key is to be present and focus on your breath. Inhale slowly and deeply through your nose. Then exhale slowly through your mouth. As you breathe, pay attention to the sensations in your body and your surroundings. Imagine you're in a movie, and you're the viewer dissecting each scene. Be an outsider looking in. This will help you detach yourself from your thoughts and emotions.

Actions, Not Emotions

Emotions are fleeting. They come and go. Usually, they're not based on logic or reason, and actions are different. Actions are based on logic and reason.

They're well thought out and planned. For that reason, they tend to be more effective than emotions.

When it comes to taking action, focus on the task at hand and do not get caught up in your emotions. Emotions have the power to hold us back. The wrong emotions can cloud our judgment and prevent us from taking action. It's normal to feel fear when you face a new or challenging task, but that doesn't mean you should let that fear stop you.

The best way to overcome your fears is to take action, regardless of how you feel. Do it as you are petrified. As long as you're taking action toward your goal, that's all that matters. The more action you take, the less power your fear will have over you. You always want to keep your emotions in check—do not avoid or hide them, but keep them tamed because when you're in control of your emotions, you're in control of your life.

Emotions impede our actions. Don't let them drive you. Only your actions should drive you. Let your actions result from logic and reasoning, not emotions. Don't be a slave to your emotions. Emotions sometimes give us a spike of energy, but more often, they will slow down or stop us. Don't get hooked on that fuel. Don't depend on that. Get up and engage in an activity. Your emotions will follow along. Create a stage for the emotion you want to be present. It will come right after.

You can't be happy all the time, and you can't be productive all the time. That's not how life works. But you can learn to control your emotions and not let them control you.

Routines, Habits, and Consistency

If you want to achieve something, put in the hard work and dedication. There are no clear-cut, super-easy shortcuts. Be consistent with your efforts, and you must also be disciplined. Many people give up too soon because they don't see results. However, results take time. Trust the process and trust that you will eventually see results if you keep working hard.

Developing proper habits and routines can help with consistency. Routines help eliminate decision fatigue and keep you on track. When you have a set routine, you don't have to waste time and energy trying to figure out what you need to do next. You just follow your routine and everything falls into place.

Routines keep us in motion. They help us take action even when we don't feel like it, and the more action you take, the more momentum you'll build. The key is to just get started. Once you get started, it becomes easier to keep going. If you have no routines, create some. Create a morning or evening ritual. It doesn't matter. A routine can rescue you in times of need. It can be your safety net, your fallback plan. Routines only work if you're consistent with them, though. So, stick with them and do not give up.

Instead of Evening Prayers

1. Do you have any plans for the upcoming weekend? If yes, move forward with your plans. If not, pick a day and fill it with events like going to brunch, a museum, a theater, or a movie. You can do it alone or with someone else. It does not matter as long as you make a plan for the whole day.

2. Do you have anything fun scheduled within the workweek? Why not spice up your life by adding fun-filled activities to an evening in the middle of the week? Is there anything you re-

ally want to do? Or any cool events happening in town soon?

3. For those who don't follow a routine, create a morning or evening schedule for yourself. Fill it with anything you fancy—but stay true to that script and every day.

13

— • —

LIE LIKE A PRO

Ever since we were children, our parents taught us that lying is bad. But what if I told you that there's nothing wrong with lying? Let's cut the bullshit. In fact, lying can be downright helpful—that's my opinion, anyway. Lying is often seen as a negative quality, but it doesn't have to be. Sometimes, lying is the best way to get what you want or need.

I follow a personal philosophy for lying: As long as I abide by my core values and the lie doesn't bring anyone pain, then I see nothing wrong with the occasional white lie. Lying can be used as a means of self-preservation or simply to make someone feel better. It all comes down to delivery and intention.

Now, I'm not saying that you should go out and start lying to people left and right—that's obviously not the answer. However, the next time you face a difficult situation, consider lying as an option. It might just be the best way to handle it.

You Don't Have to Tell the Truth All the Time

Sounds like a weird nugget of advice, doesn't it? But it's true. You don't always have to tell the truth. In fact, sometimes it's better if you don't. Sometimes the whole *If you don't have something nice to say, then don't say anything at all* spiel doesn't work. If telling the truth might hurt somebody's feelings or get you into trouble, and there's no way to avoid the situation, it's okay to embellish the truth a little. It's not always easy to do, but not every thought needs to be said. You don't have to own that "blunt friend" title. If you can't say something nice, say nothing at all, is especially true with family and friends.

If your friend doesn't look good in a particular outfit but they love it and feel confident, there's no need to point out that the outfit is unflattering. It's not your place, and it'll only make your friend feel bad. The same goes for family. If your Aunt Gertrude asks if you like her new hairdo, of course you're going to say you do—even if it's the worst haircut you've ever seen. If you say no, arguments might ensue, and feelings might erupt. It's just a little white lie, and it'll save everybody a lot of grief in the long run.

You also don't have to tell the truth about yourself all the time. It's okay to keep your personal business under wraps. As long as there is no harm done, why would it matter? It's up to you what to share and in what capacity. Or perhaps a stranger on a plane asks you personal questions about your life. There is no need for honesty. You can tell them as many fictitious details as you wish. You owe nothing to that stranger or anyone else for that matter. In fact, it could be really unsafe to be an open book. I wouldn't overshare with strangers. Small talk with a cab driver or a random person at a bar could put you in a really uncomfortable situation. Lies can save lives.

Lies Can Be Beneficial and Help You Achieve Goals

As I said before, sometimes lying is the best way to get what you want or help you achieve a goal. Let's say, for example, that you're trying to get a job. The interview process can be daunting, and sometimes it seems like the odds are stacked against you. You might not believe you have the right qualifications or be concerned about the behavioral interview questions. Many people get nervous and can't think of an example. However, before the interview, you can think of scenarios and answers to questions beforehand.

For instance, if you know they're going to ask for an example of when you had to problem-solve, you can smooth the edges of your answers with a few white lies. Maybe your old job doesn't have a direct correlation. In that case, you can embellish on a similar problem to be more relatable to the job and the interviewer.

Honestly, interviewers are always asking a lot of bullshit questions, such as, "Give me an example of a time you saved the world, a time you were proud of your achievement, and a time you brought tremendous revenue to your company." So, sometimes lying is a good fit to get your name in someone's mouth. You might just be able to convince the interviewer that you're the best candidate for the job. Just lie.

In this case, lying can help you get your foot in the door and land the job you want. You're not lying about your qualifications; you're simply retelling the story in a manner that appeases the interviewer. In this way, lying can actually be a good thing. The concern is the intention behind the lies. Are you intending to hurt someone? Are you trying to take advantage of the situation? If not, then a little white lie might just be what you need.

Lies Can Get You Out of Unpleasant Situations

Have you ever been on an awkward date with someone you're not interested in? Or been stuck in a conversation with someone you can't stand? We've all been there, and sometimes, the best way to get out of an unpleasant situation is to tell a lie. It's not the nicest thing to do, but sometimes it's necessary. If you're on a date with someone, and you're not enjoying your time together, say you have an early meeting, and you're going to call it a night. Then you can make your escape. If you don't want to go to your friend's party, you might say you're not feeling well, so you can stay home.

In social situations, it's not always easy to be honest. Sometimes we lie out of politeness. We don't want to hurt somebody's feelings by telling them the truth. Those little white lies can save us from a lot of discomforts. In these cases, lying can actually be a good thing.

Lies Can Help You Avoid Conflict

Sometimes the best way to avoid conflict is to lie. If somebody asks you if you like their newborn's photograph and you really don't, it's probably best to lie and say you do. An argument over something so trivial is unnecessary. Sometimes, it's just not worth it to tell the truth. If somebody asks you if you think their wedding dress is "on fleek" and you really don't, it's probably best to say yes. It's not worth creating an uncomfortable situation over something so minor. In these cases, it's best to just bite your tongue and keep the peace.

Don't Be Afraid to Tell the Truth

Yes, while I'm advocating the occasional stretch of truth, that doesn't mean you should lie all the time. Telling the truth is the best policy in many situations. For example, if your manager asks you about the project you are working on, and you are falling behind due to reasons that are out of your control, or you are going through tough times outside of work, it's better to come clean. The same goes for family and friends. If your parents ask you how school is going, and you're failing all your classes, it's time for a heart-to-heart talk. In these situations, honesty is the best policy because more pain or struggles can arise without it. You would rather not lie to the people who care about you or genuinely want your help—it'll only make the situation worse in the long run.

However, sometimes we struggle because we would rather not disappoint others or hurt someone else's feelings. Nonetheless, you should feel equally comfortable and confident in the truth and the lie. For example, if you're dating someone and you realize they're not the person you're looking for, don't ghost them. Tell them the truth. Follow your best interests or gut feeling and do it with confidence.

Sometimes we lie because we're afraid of the truth. We don't want to face reality, so we tell ourselves little white lies instead. We don't want to hurt others or be judged. However, that's not a healthy practice. If you find yourself having to lie to make yourself feel better, it might be time to take a step back and reassess the situation. Maybe it's time for a change. Lying is a complicated issue, and there's no easy answer. If you have a truth that you really believe you should share, then share it. If it's coming from a place of love and understanding, share the truth.

Get Your Facts Straight

One last note: If you're going to lie, make sure you get your facts straight. Being caught in a lie is the worst. If you're caught in a lie, it'll be harder for people to trust you in the future, and that's not a good place to be. You'll have to backpedal and cover your tracks, which can make it worse. This is generally why most people avoid lying in the first place. One lie can easily turn into a web of lies, and it's not worth it in the end. However, if you absolutely have to lie, make sure you get your story straight.

What did you tell the person? How did you tell them? What was their reaction? You need to remember all the details of the lie to keep from getting caught. Luckily, if it was a small lie like telling your friend they looked good in the dress when they really didn't, you can probably get away with forgetting the details. If it was a bigger lie, you need to remember all the details, so you don't get caught. For instance, if you told your boss you were sick at home when you really were partying in Aruba, then you have to be careful and smart with receipts and details so you don't get caught.

Why Are People Afraid to Lie?

So, if lying can be so beneficial, why are people afraid to do it? I don't understand why. I understand some lies can hurt others, but that's in a general sense. If a person has bad intentions, then they will use lies to their advantage to hurt others. On the other hand, if we're talking about the little white lies that we tell to save ourselves or others from discomfort, then I don't understand why people are so afraid of them. I think people are just too honest for their own good. They need to lighten up and learn how to lie without feeling guilty about it. It's not a dangerous action—maybe a little offensive, but it's just a part of life.

We're not children anymore. Our parents will not punish us for lying. We need to learn how to use lies to our advantage. If the lie does not affect the person you are lying to in any way, what makes it bad? Get this fear of punishment off your head. Lie if you need to. It's not a big deal. Just don't make it a habit, and try not to lie about something that could really hurt somebody. Other than that, I say go for it! The next time you're in an uncomfortable situation or you need to get out of something, don't be afraid to lie.

Earlier in the year, I had a conversation with my friend, Elizabeth, about adultery. I'm monogamous, and to me, adultery is an unforgivable act. My pride, self-respect, and values are totally against cheating. I cannot forgive a partner for stepping out on a relationship. However, I do understand that circumstances could be different—many scenarios are possible. People make mistakes. Other people can also help or push people to make mistakes. It doesn't make the cheater any better or feel less guilty, but we all can meet the Devil and fall for a sin. However, some of us do learn from our missteps.

So, I told Elizabeth that, theoretically, if my partner is not a pathological cheater and made a terrible mistake (that they know they would never repeat), I wouldn't want to know about it. If I found out, the relationship would be over—regardless of how apologetic they were. They would have to accept that I would be hurt and walk away. If I know, we cannot recover from it.

However, we had opposing views. She wanted to understand my point, so she asked me, "Don't you think the bitter truth is better than being lied to? How can you be sure they won't cheat again?"

While she has a valid point at its core, I disagree. As I stated, this would be their first fuckup. I believe some of us can and do learn from our mistakes. Not everyone is a recidivist. If I'm being lied to—because someone intends to protect my feelings—great! I don't need to know the fucking truth because it will only mess everything up. I'll get upset, I'll get mad, and I will leave. If they are not going to make the same mistake again, there's no reason to act funny. If your relationship is healthy, you will sense when something is off if there's more to it.

The problem is when people who rarely cheat make that mistake, the burden of the guilt is unbearable for them. Sometimes they need to get it off their chest. Even if they know it will lead to the end of everything, they will still tell their partner and hope for the best. To me, that is selfish. They did it to release their pain but then placed it on another. If you made a mistake—your first and only one—and you know your partner has no clue about it, then protect your relationship. Protect your partner from learning the truth at all costs.

Your partner gave you their heart. You can't break it just because you fucked up, and cannot bear the guilt. Straight up: That is your mistake; that is your fuckup, and you have to live with it. Now it's your job to protect the love of your life from pain and save the relationship. This example is the perfect situation when the truth could do more damage than good.

I know it's a personal and controversial topic. I'm certainly not advocating that we should cheat on our partners and then hide it, so it will be okay. In my opinion, for my personal relationship, if I'm invested, happy, and love you—don't you dare ruin it for me. If you still love me but fucked up once, make sure it won't happen again and protect me from finding this out until the day I die.

Instead of Evening Prayers

Have you ever been in that awkward situation where you had to introduce yourself to others, knowing you probably would never see them again? This scenario could be an excellent opportunity to master your lying skills.

I recall being in Alaska and visiting a reindeer farm. The tour guide put us in a circle and asked everyone to say who they were, where they came from, and what they do for a living. It was awkward, tiring, and unnecessary. I did not want to share my personal information, so I lied. I told the group that my name was Alex, I lived in D.C., and I worked as an accountant. Try it the next time you are in a similar situation, like a meet and greet or party with strangers. Not only is it good practice, but it's also loads of fun.

14

THE SUGAR BABY AWARD

Far too often, we believe that we have to live up to society's standards in order to be successful. We think we need to have a certain job, earn a specific amount of money, own a particular house, and drive a good car. However, success is not defined by what society tells us. Success is defined by our own personal goals and aspirations. So, even if you're a sugar baby, don't let anyone tell you that's a silly occupation. You can be the best damn sugar baby in the world, and you will be successful.

Don't Look Down on Others for Having a Less Traditional Career Path

Some people want to be doctors or lawyers, and that's great. However, not everyone wants to have a traditional career path, and that's okay too! Some people want to be the next Larry David or Rihanna. Some want to perform in a circus, while others want to be a "sugar baby" and reap the benefits from a wealthy sugar mama or sugar daddy. No matter what your career aspirations are, don't let anyone tell you that you're not successful because you don't have a traditional job. You can be successful in any field that you put your mind to. Your success is defined by your personal goals, not by society's standards.

Someone's less traditional career path doesn't mean they're not successful. Traditional is subjective and overrated anyway. Live up to your own standards, and don't let anyone else dictate what success means to you. You can be successful in whatever career you choose, as long as you're the best at what you do. Everyone's journey is unique, and what works for one person may not work for another. Don't look down on someone for having a less traditional career path. Instead, support them and be happy about their success. There are no prestigious career paths. There are happy career paths and non-happy ones. Period. The bottom line is that you should do what makes you happy and not let anyone else dictate your success.

My friend Adam used to work as an attorney. One day, he was overwhelmed and complained about how much he hated his job. The corporate culture and toxic legal environment were eating away at his soul.

He was working long hours, and that resulted in around-the-clock stress. He had a new career in mind: A barista. However, it's a low-paying job, and he believed his support system would look down upon him. They would think him stupid for giving up a solid, high-paying career for what many would consider an entry-level, dead-end job that he's overqualified for.

I was mystified that he had a new passion, but the social pressure was too heavy for him to shake off. So, I told him, "You don't have to be just a barista. You can be a star barista and be the best in your hood, town, state, or even country. You can own a coffee shop." It took him more than a year to process this and agree with what I said, but when he did, he started working part-time as a barista on the weekends. He loved it so much that he ended up resigning from his position at the firm, and eventually, he opened his own small, cute coffee shop. Now, he's happier than ever, and he's doing what he loves. Also, he's successful.

Don't let anyone else determine your success. You are the only one who knows what makes you happy. So, pursue your dreams, and don't let anyone stop you from being the best at what you do. Adam's changing his career path didn't make him unsuccessful. He's happy, and that's all that matters. Therefore, don't look down on others for having a less traditional career path. You never know what someone is going through or what their journey looks like. Support them and be happy about their success. After all, success is subjective, and everyone's definition of it is different.

The Number One Regret: Not Being Authentic

At the end of our lives, we all have regrets—places we wish we had visited, people we never apologized to, or risks we never took. Do you know one of the biggest regrets people have on their deathbeds? Not being true to themselves. Changing who they were to appease other people, giving up on hopes and dreams to please others—that is their number one regret.

Everyone wants to be loved and accepted. We put on different masks, pretending to be someone we're not, just to fit in. We change our interests, the way we dress, or the way we talk to fall in line with those around us. However, in doing so, we lose sight of who we are. We become someone else's idea of who we should be, a mold created by our surroundings, and that is not living. That is not an authentic life.

Can you imagine living your whole life traveling to places you have no passion for? Or working in a career your entire life because you want to impress certain people, or because you would rather not disappoint a person? How does wearing a mask every day, hiding your true self, help you? It would be miserable. How sad is that—to not own your own life and live for someone else? You may not even realize you're doing it. It's easy to get lost and end up living someone else's life, but it's not worth it.

It is not worth sacrificing your dreams, hopes, and goals just to please others. You are the only one who has to live with the consequences of your actions. Only you will be by your side at the end of your life. You should never give up on your dreams or change who you are to please someone else. You are the only one who has to live with the regrets of a lifetime.

Only Two More Generations Will Remember You—Unless You Become the Next Mozart

In the grand scheme of things, we are but a blip on the radar. We live our lives day in and day out, and then we die. That's it. We are born, we live, and then we die. After we die, only a handful of people will remember us. Your great-grandparents are probably dead, and your grandparents will be gone eventually too. In a few generations, no one will remember you.

That's just the way it is. Unless you become the next Mozart or Einstein, you will be forgotten. So, what are you so afraid of? Even if you were striving for those ambitions, you would never achieve them by following society's rules. People would likely look at you as if you were insane for wanting to become the next Mozart—would you let that stop you from trying?

Be true to yourself. Don't be afraid to live your life the way you want it to be. Don't be afraid to be your true self. We only have one life to live, and we're all going to die. That's a fact, so make it count. The only person you should be afraid to fail is yourself.

Don't Be Afraid to Switch Lanes

Do you know how many years it takes to become a lawyer? What about a doctor? These are highly respected professions that come with a lot of responsibilities. My friend Adam, from the story above, had to go to college for four years and then law school for another three. He had thousands of dollars in student loans to pay off. After all of that, he was still working long hours with little spare time. It's no wonder he resigned from his job and became a barista. He wasn't happy with what he was doing and wanted to do something different.

Sometimes, we can get so caught up in the expectations of others that we forget to pursue our own happiness. We get caught up in the investment—the money, time, and energy we've put into something—that we forget to ask ourselves if we're actually happy. We think we have to stay on the same path we've always been on. It's okay to take a risk by switching lanes and making a drastic change. Being a lawyer doesn't mean you can't become a barista, and if you're a barista, that doesn't mean you can't become a lawyer. It's never too late to try a different path.

It's normal for our likes and dislikes to change five years down the road—to lose interest in something and switch our focus to something new. We switch our hobbies, clothes, cars, and even homes. Why can't the same apply to our careers? Don't fall into the trap of feeling invested in what you have been doing. It doesn't matter how long you have been doing your job. If you are dying to try a new career or have a new passion, then drop what you're doing and try the new gig.

You can take smart steps, as my friend did if that makes you more comfortable. You can transition safely and at a slower speed. Put your blinker on, check your mirrors, and organize your affairs. You don't have to jeopardize yourself, but as I said, don't give up on a goal because you have already invested your time in something else. You are still taking all the knowledge and experience that you gained from your prior passion with you. It's not going anywhere—it stays with you. It's yours.

If you feel miserable doing what you do now, wouldn't you want to ease your pain? Imagine an injured person refusing medical help because they've been injured for a while already. They've already put time and energy into living with their injuries, so there's no point. It's nonsense, isn't it? You should act in your own interest. You don't have an obligation to be the person you were five minutes ago, let alone five years ago.

You don't want that kind of pressure anymore? Want to be a stay-at-home mom or a freelance writer? That's perfectly okay too! Your career path is not set in stone. If you're not happy with what you're doing, then it's okay to switch lanes. You don't have to stay on the same path because you've invested in it.

It's never too late to try something new. If you're not happy with your current situation, then do something about it. Life is too short to stay unhappy. Change the course of everything if you feel like it. It's your life. You are the author.

Instead of Evening Prayers

1. Do you have a passion? Are you actively searching for one? Try to discover it by exposing yourself to different subjects that interest you. Do some serious research. Passion discovery is a big—probably the most important—project of our lives. Also, keep in mind, passions come and go. What worked yesterday may not work today. Explore.

2. Do you truly love where you are in life? Do you enjoy what you are doing career-wise? If not, why not?

3. Imagine yourself at 90 years old in a hospital bed. You're ready to go to the other side. What regrets do you have? What do you think you would've done differently? What do you think the 90-year-old version you would tell the "today" you?

15

BFF

What is a best friend? A best friend is someone with whom you have a strong emotional connection. You enjoy spending time with them, and they make you feel good about yourself. They are someone you can rely on. They are there for you during good and bad times.

A friend is someone who understands you, someone you can be yourself around without feeling judged. A friend is someone who makes you laugh, someone who dries your tears when you're sad. Friends are an important part of our lives, and we should cherish them.

Friends are all the people you care about. This can include your parents, cousins, aunts, uncles, coworkers, and so on. Some people aren't close to their family. If that's true in your case, don't beat yourself up for it. Some people find a family through their friends.

Best Friends Are Investments

A best friend is someone worth investing in. They are someone who you want to keep in your life for the long haul. You may not always agree with them, but you know that they have your best interests at heart. You can count on them, no matter what.

This quality is not applicable to regular, casual friends. This chapter is not about them. You can have as many acquaintances (or friends, as some people call them) as you wish. BFFs are on an entirely different level. They are your ride or die, your confidante, you're everything. They know you on the "ocean deep" level.

Like many people, I used to believe the more friends I had, the better, but eventually, quantity always hurts quality. Today, I see friends as priceless investments—of my being, mostly. As we spoke about in Chapter 11, they're part of my stock market. I don't view them this way because I'm materialistic and want what they can offer me. No. I want to see good people—people who love me and on whom I can rely on and trust—beside me. Furthermore, I would like to give and feel love. I'm selective about whom I can start a deep friendship with, and honestly, I never look to make best friends.

For me, best friends happen organically. The moment I realize we share the same core values and we vibe well, I know this person is special to me. As I said, best friends are an investment—forever. The relationship is filled with enormous responsibility and hard work. It's not just a title or label. I want to be available for my BFFs.

I would like to be a high-quality BFF. When you have a lot of friends, it's impossible to connect with them all. So, you have to be responsible if you are committing to a deep friendship. It's a long-term investment—a lifetime investment if both of you are lucky. Treat it seriously. I'm not saying to be paranoid and fret about what you say or do. No, that's not what being responsible means. It means being aware that this is a serious relationship in which a lot is at stake: Your secrets, your sanity, and your life.

What does being a responsible friend entail? It means you are present when your BFF needs you. You don't ghost them when they need you the most. You don't make up excuses like, "I'm too busy," "I have work," or "I'm tired." If you can't be there for them emotionally, you should at least let them know you're thinking of them. You send a text, make a phone call, or, even better, you show up. Responsible friends are there for each other until the Earth stops turning.

Personal Connections and Compatibility Is Crucial

Above, I mentioned I'm selective about people who can become my best friend. Let's be real and not sugar-coat bullshit. It's impossible, and I'd say even preposterous, to build a friendship with a person who's of an utterly different breed from you. I'm not referring to income or social class here. I mean someone who doesn't share the same mental, intellectual, and spiritual alignment. The only exception to this rule is a friendship with your pet. They will love you no matter how much of an asshole you are.

Since best friends are on a different level, if you don't have that connection or open-mindedness, the friendship won't work. I need to discuss a wide range of topics with my BFFs, and the judgment needs to be minimal. I need to know we can dive deep into context and intellectualize the challenges in our lives. It feels amazing when we can engage in stimulating conversations. If I can't have these types of chats with my BFFs, the friendship will not work for me. We'd lack compatibility and run out of things to talk about quickly. When this happens, the friendship fizzles out.

I need to evaluate a person when I first meet them. A connection needs to be clear between us. I need to feel a particular vibe to believe we can become amazing friends, and that person needs to respond with the same intentions. Only then am I down to build a friendship.

What catches me in people mostly is talent. If that person is talented, I'm sold. It can be any talent. They can have creative, business, or intellectual talent. They can be humorous, empathetic, or talented professionals—anything that brings that spark out of them. Talent makes people interesting. The spark creates a fire that makes them driven and bright. I like to be immersed in talented people.

Talents can vary and be diverse—you don't want to surround yourself with people that are boring, and you learn nothing from them. Friends should learn from each other. You teach your friends, and they teach you in return. If you don't feel like you're growing as a person because of your friendship, it's not worth it. Friendship should make you want to be a better person. Having goals and dreams is something that I look for in my BFFs too.

However, even with the connection and great conversations, another factor determines whether or not I'm going to take the friendship to the next level. It all boils down to trust. Do I feel I can trust this person? With my secrets? My life? If not, the friendship is over before it even starts. Friendship, like any relationship, is built on trust. If that foundation is not there, the friendship will crumble.

Don't Count Favors

Remember what I said about friends being an investment? Investment doesn't only mean money. It means time, emotion, and effort. If you keep track of what you do for your friends and what they do for you, it will only backfire. The friendship will become one-sided, and sooner or later, your friends will get fed up with it. Instead of keeping track of who did what, focus on being a good friend and being there for your friends when they need you. Invest in your friends out of love and kindness.

Investments are priceless. Your friends are priceless, but there does need to be an investment. Just as you have a high and low buyout when purchasing stocks, you should have them with your BFFs. You shouldn't count favors because that is your investment. What you do for them should be priceless, a favor without expecting something. However, you create the boundaries of how much and what you're willing to provide. Refer to Chapter 4 and apply some border control.

There should be an invisible line you need to feel and pay attention to. Your friends are family, and while you don't want to be taken advantage of, you also don't want to cut off a good friend out of pride. Staunch friends are hard to find, so when you find one, hold on to them tightly. These friends will be there for you through thick and thin. They're the ones you can count on, no matter what. They're the ones who will help you up when you're down and be there to celebrate your victories. These are the friends that you want to keep for life.

Life Hack: Go Traveling Together First

Honestly, this can apply to any relationship you're considering investing in—from partners to friends. If your new friendship is going well and you think you might shorten the boundaries, go on a trip together before really letting them into your inner world. Traveling is a great compatibility test. Traveling with someone is like marriage—a mini life. If you get along well, it's a prominent sign you will probably be great friends. If not, reconsider.

I've noticed needy or annoying people can't hide their true selves during trips. So, if you want to find a good friend that you can trust, go on a trip together. It will show you everything you need to know about that person. If your new friend ruins your vacation, it's a vibrant red flag. Either say "goodbye" to that person or leave the friendship at the pre-trip level and don't fall into any mental traps.

Be a Cheerleader

Recently, while I was scrolling on TikTok, I saw a video with a man listening to sad music in the background and saying something like, "Want to see who your true friends are? Go through Hell and see who's walking by your side." While he had a point, I immediately cringed and rolled my eyes. He was missing a few key points.

First, the man, like many other people, romanticized being dramatic. What's up with all the drama? Why would you tell someone to "go through Hell" when we should do our best to avoid it at all costs? Second, success exposes a person's true self—whether you're on the receiving end or lacking. Pay attention to how the surrounding people react to winning.

Genuine friends are not just always interested in your being and your business; they are always happy about your success. Loyal friends will genuinely cheer for you and celebrate you and your achievements. Loyal friends want you to succeed. True friends understand that it's not just your success; it's your group's success. With more people succeeding, everyone can win.

Success brings success. They want to see successful people around them. They want to see you thriving. Those people are your genuine friends, not someone who wants you to be bitter. So, choose how you want to discover your true friends. Do you want to go through Hell and see who's at your side, or do you want to grab a ladder and keep climbing up to the stars?

On the other hand, cheer and support your people too. Don't just be a taker; also be a giver. When you see your friends succeed, be just as happy for them, if not more. Loyal friends are always happy to see each other win. Celebrate their success as your own. If your friend starts a business, be their first customer. Support them in any way you can. It should be a pleasure for you to pay for your friend's goods or services.

Don't Expect Discounts

Don't ask for discounts. Don't ask for free shit. It's disrespectful. Your friend will probably treat you special anyway. If they don't, then that's okay too. Tell your friends how proud you are when they achieve their goals. If your friend is making their first steps toward their goals, encourage them. Go to their first performance, attend their graduation, sit in on their first hearing, and support them in any way you can. Don't forget, though, if someone does not appreciate your work or success, fuck them. They are not mature enough to be your BFF.

For example, I'm not close friends with Tony, but he's a nice guy and connected to my inner circle. We keep in touch occasionally, and recently, he learned I was working on this book. The first question out of his mouth was, "Would you send me a free copy when you finish?" Immediately, I blurted, "No!"

Tony was taken aback as he blinked momentarily before uttering, "Oh, wow. Someone is being very cheap." I was a little insulted that he didn't understand the politics behind my reasoning, so I offered him a free coaching session and broke everything down. I told him,

I respect my labor, and I don't work for free. If you are not treating your labor the same, you might want to reevaluate your personal value. This is my first book, and I'm excited to share my work with the world. My friends are excited, just as I am, and they can't wait to show their support and appreciation. They want to buy copies of my book and share how proud they are of me with the world. If you don't have money to purchase my book, I'd be happy to gift it to you, but it seems like you immediately saw it as an advantage, as a freebie.

To help connect the dots, I asked him what his dream was. Tony wanted to open up a spa retreat, so I painted a picture:

Imagine that you worked so hard to put together your first business. You're excited to welcome your first customers and earn your first dollar. As you're waiting for paying customers to arrive, your family and circle of friends enter. Immediately, they ask you for free services, like a free massage or pedicure. Wouldn't that ruin your experience and excitement? That's not support—that's an advantage. Now, imagine the same people wanting to come to support your business by becoming your first paying customers. How does that feel? Empowering, right? Of course, you would likely give them special treatment, including a family and friend discount, but you get my point.

Tony understood. I'm happy to report that he's now one of my book's biggest supporters, and I plan to return the favor when he opens a retreat. However, that leads me to my next point.

Friends Deserve Special Treatment

I know I just said, "Don't give your friends free shit," but your friends are special people who deserve more than just the bare minimum. So, show them how much you care! We're humans, and sometimes we take each other for granted. Or we get wrapped up in our own lives and forget to show them how much they mean to us. However, a little special treatment doesn't have to be big or expensive. Remember to be thoughtful and intentional in your actions, and your friends will know how much you care.

Do a little extra for your friends. If you usually send a birthday text to others, your BFFs deserve a call instead or even a surprise visit. If sometimes you get pleasure from treating your acquaintances to a cup of coffee, then treat your BFFs to a cake. By taking this extra step, you both will feel superior. Let your besties know how special they are to you and how lucky you feel to have them in your life.

Communication Is Key

Going on outings or bonding over hobbies is one way to show your friends you care, but communication is also key. Whether you're catching up over coffee or just shooting the breeze through text, be present and engaged in the conversation. Listen to what they have to say and take an interest in their lives. Ask them questions and follow up. Showing that you care about them and their lives will go a long way in showing how much you appreciate them as friends.

Also, always talk to your friends if something is bothering you about the relationship. They care about you, so don't bottle up your emotions. Don't disregard a problem and let it build until it becomes something serious. Most of the time, the problem you might see is just a misunderstanding or miscommunication. If you're not happy or the relationship feels off, talk to your friend immediately. Friendships are built on trust and communication, so keep the lines of communication open. The two of you should be comfortable with open dialogue, and good communication will only strengthen your friendship.

Reliability

A good friend is someone you can rely on, which means you also have to be reliable to be a good friend.

Reliability is a magnificent quality any friend can have, and this quality forms strong friendships. If you know your friend is reliable, you will feel more comfortable confiding in them and sharing your life with them. You will feel better about asking them for favors and advice. A reliable friend is someone you can count on to keep their word and follow through on their promises. They're there for you when you need them, and they're always happy to help.

Being reliable doesn't mean being available 24/7; it means giving and helping your friend when you are emotionally and physically capable. It means keeping your word. You can build your reliable character in your friend's eyes through clear communication. If you aren't able to deliver something, you better tell them the truth instead of saying yes and then trying to get off the hook. People will appreciate it more.

If you're constantly flaking on your friends or canceling plans, they'll think you're unreliable. If they believe you're not reliable, they'll question your friendship. You need to be a good friend if you want to have solid friends. Your level of availability will depend on your lifestyle and obligations, but make sure your friends know they can count on you when they need you. Your availability should be higher for your friends—they should know that it is and feel important.

They should know that they can reach you at any time if needed. The outside world doesn't matter. You can be as unreachable as you want to the outside world. The wider the gap in your availability between your friends and outsiders, the more valuable and precious your time is going to feel for your friends. They will see how unreachable you are for others, but you are always there for them. It's touching.

Share an Experience Instead of a Lecture

People hate being lectured. We're adults, and most of us aren't in school anymore, so lectures are the last thing we want to hear. If you think there's room for improvement in a friend, there's nothing wrong with offering some advice, but avoid lecturing them. Instead, share an experience with them. If you've been through something similar, tell them about it. Use your experience to help them see the situation from a different perspective. Sharing an experience shows that you're trying to help them, not judge them. You empathize with them. You've been there before.

It will be much more effective than lecturing them. Lectures usually make people defensive and less likely to listen to what you have to say. A staunch friend is someone who sees the pain in your eyes while everyone else still believes in the smile on your face. They know your history and still love you. They notice the potential in you, even when you don't see it in yourself. So, be a genuine friend. See the potential in your friends, love them for their history, and be there for them when they need you. Prompt them to be better, but gently.

Friends Grow Apart

As time goes on, friends grow apart. People change, and their lives take them in different directions. Developing and growing at the same pace with someone is rare. Sometimes we significantly outgrow the people we were friends with. Sometimes we live far away, and the ties loosen.

This occurrence is natural, but then you might stop enjoying each other's company or start enjoying it less than before. This might cause feelings of guilt or obligation. However, you shouldn't be afraid of feeling this way. You don't have to become enemies, but you can suspend your friendship or limit it for an undefined period.

It's fine to grow apart from your friends. You should never feel obligated to maintain a relationship with someone if it doesn't feel right. Forcing a relationship will only lead to resentment. If you feel like you're out-growing your friends or if the friendship is no longer serving you, it's okay to let it go.

You don't have to exile the person completely. If you have a shared history and happy memories, you can keep them in your life in a different capacity. At some point, you might match again and be able to vibe at the same or higher frequencies. This "break" can look different for everyone. Some people stop talking to each other. Others keep the relationship afloat with a "Happy Birthday" and a "Happy Holidays."

Some simply talk less and reduce interactions. What you choose doesn't matter. Don't feel obligated to stay invested in a friendship you don't want to maintain. I understand that we have friends from childhood that we grew up with in our close circles. In that situation, I'd try to preserve every beautiful moment I remember about the friendship. I'd preserve and cherish that friendship, but I wouldn't force myself to be around someone whose company I no longer enjoy. It doesn't matter how much time we invest in a person or rela-tionship. Clear some space for other people—for peo-ple who will bring you more joy.

Your life should mostly be about you and your well-be-ing. You should care about your happiness, and when it comes to adult talk, you shouldn't be terrified of hurting someone's feelings. Chances are, the other person feels the same way too. However, instead of being honest, you both keep playing this game of putting your time and energy somewhere else. Just put your friendship on hold until further notice.

If a Person Doesn't Show Interest in You—They're Not Worth Your Time

The problem with making friends as an adult is that not everyone is interested in being friends with you. They may want your services or status. They might simply want more company because of their own status. Choosing whom to pick and keep as friends is hard, but you need to be discerning. You don't want to waste your time on someone who's not interested in being your friend. If someone doesn't show interest in you or your life, they're not worth your time. Plenty of people are out there who would love to be friends with you. So, don't waste your time on someone who doesn't reciprocate your interest.

Toxic Friendships

A toxic friendship is a one-sided relationship where you are constantly giving, and the other person is always taking. These friendships often leave you feeling drained, used, and unappreciated. If you find yourself in a friendship like this, it might be time to reevaluate the relationship.

If you are dealing with toxic friendships and don't want to abandon them because you feel invested, you should know that it's not a healthy relationship. It doesn't matter how much you have invested in that friendship. Carrying some stinky shit in your hands because you have been carrying it for so long makes no sense. Throw it away immediately. Clean your hands and leave your hand available for some beautiful flower who wants you and deserves you. A toxic friendship is not genuine and is not based on love, trust, or respect.

Jealousy

Jealousy is often the root of many problems in friendships. It can lead to feelings of insecurity, competition, and even resentment. This quality is one I notice a lot in toxic friendships. People are jealous of their friends having other friends, which, in my opinion, is wrong on multiple levels.

The loving heart is limitless by definition. You shouldn't be afraid if your friend has another friend. It doesn't mean that your friend loves you any less. The more friends somebody has, the more love they have to give. Don't be alarmed if their relationship is exclusive. They may have something really intimate and special, which is normal for us to crave.

If you are jealous of your friend, try to replace it with curiosity. Learn more about that friend of theirs. Ask about their relationship. Be happy that your friend has multiple friendships because it only says good things about your BFF. Your BFF making friends means they're likable to other humans, which means your judgment of people was on point when you signed up to be their bestie.

A highly liked BFF means they have good personal qualifications. I love when my friends meet and get along. It's a network within a network, which can be helpful if one of your friends can benefit someone else you know. If this is the case in your circle, recommend them to each other. It shows substantial support from your end. When your friends are friends with each other, it's amazing.

If you ever felt jealous of your friend, ask yourself why. Often, jealousy is based on insecurity or feelings of inadequacy. If you can't be happy about your friend's accomplishments, chances are you're not thrilled for them at all. You're jealous. If you're jealous of your friend, try to change the way you think. Instead of thinking about what you don't have, focus on what you do have. Be happy for your friend and try to celebrate their successes with them. If you find that you're still struggling with jealousy, it might be time to take a step back and reassess your friendship.

Instead of Evening Prayers

1. Close your eyes and think about each of your best friends individually. What emotions does each bring? Are they positive? Does your BFF circle need to be reshaped?

2. How do you support your BFFs? Do you know their goals and dreams?

3. When was the last time you told those BFFs how much you love and appreciate them? Can you reach out to them now and let them know how you feel?

16

You're Gonna Be Fine

We all have fears—fears of the unknown, of failure, and of not being good enough. Most of the time, these fears are nothing more than figments in our minds. Fear is an emotion, and our emotions are often irrational. So, what do we do when faced with our fears? Do we let them control us and dictate our lives? Or do we face them head-on and show them who the boss is? The answer is, of course, the latter.

Fears are meant to be conquered, not coddled. When we give in to our fears, we only give them power over us, but when we confront them, we take our power back. Holding on to these fears does nothing but hold us back from enjoying life. It's time to let them go. You're gonna be fine. Whatever you're afraid of, you can handle it. You've got this.

Eight Percent of Our Worries Come True

According to the WCNC Staff, 8% of the things we worry about happening to us will actually occur (WCNC Staff, 2019). Out of all the events that we worry about, only 8% actually come to pass. The other 92% is just wasted time worrying about things that will never happen. So, why do we do it? Worrying is a natural human emotion. It's our brain's way of trying to protect us from danger. We worry about our fears, but sometimes, our brain gets it wrong.

It mistakes a harmless situation for a dangerous one, which can lead to anxiety. It's our brain overreacting to a situation, and when we let anxiety control us, it can have a negative impact on our lives. Worrying is like a rocking chair; it gives you something to do but doesn't get you anywhere. So, why waste your time worrying about something that may never happen? Why let your fears control you when there's a 92% chance that bad things will never happen? It's time to take your power back and face your fears head-on.

Fear Is a Survival Instinct

Fear is a natural human emotion that protects us from danger. It's an evolutionary survival instinct that has helped our species survive for millennia. When we face a dangerous situation, our brain releases a hormone called cortisol. This hormone makes us feel fear. Fear is a natural response to danger, and it's meant to help us survive. However, in today's world, we are not faced with the same dangers as our ancestors.

We don't have the same worries about protecting ourselves against wild animals or fighting for food. Yet, our brain still reacts to certain situations as if we are in danger. So, how do we overcome this? We reclaim our power and confront those fears.

Fears Never Go Away

Facing our fears is not easy, but it's necessary if we want to live our best lives. Our fears will never go away. They don't disappear. You can't fight them and win. The only way to deal with them is to face them. The goal is not to get rid of your fears but to learn how to deal with them. You should acknowledge that you have a fear and understand that your fear is not reality. It's just an emotion, and emotions are irrational. They don't always make sense.

Fear will never disappear because it's an emotion we regularly feel. Learn how to deal with it—control it. Then you have to take action despite your fear. Face your fears head-on. You do what you're afraid of, even though it's terrifying. Embrace and understand your fears; get close to them.

Fight or Flight

The fight-or-flight response isn't limited to survival tasks like hunting, camping, or running away from a dangerous animal. It also occurs when we're confronted with circumstances that make us feel uncomfortable or anxious, like public speaking, going on a first date, or interviewing for a job. In these situations, our brain perceives the situation as threatening and releases cortisol to help us deal with the threat.

We are physiologically preparing ourselves to either fight the threat or run away from it. In most cases, the threat is not actually dangerous. It's just something that makes us feel anxious. When we let our anxiety control us, it can have a negative impact on our lives. You always have a choice: Either leave your fear behind and keep being bothered by it, or face it and try to figure it out.

Fears Stop You From Dope Experiences

Think about your top 10 fears. Perhaps you're afraid of heights or open waters. Maybe you're afraid of large animals or flying in an airplane. Now, think about all the activities you would miss out on if you let your fears control you. You would never experience the thrill of bungee jumping off a bridge. You would never get to see the world from a bird's-eye view. You would never meet new people or try new challenges. Fears stop you from living your best life. They hold you back from experiencing all the wonderful benefits that life offers.

Your fears are just imaginary thoughts in your head that are stopping you from living your best life. They could limit you, but they're not real, and they're definitely not worth missing out on dope experiences. You are the only one who should have such power over your life.

I used to fear heights. I still do, but now I can handle my fear. A few years ago, before I would get on a plane, I would lose my touch with the ground, my knees would tremble, my vision would go dark, and I felt dizzy. I'm still scared, but I'm in control. I acknowledge my fear. Without losing the power of my mental and physical state, I can process it. Statistics show that flying is one of the safest ways to travel, and I know that. When your fears are based on real circumstances, you can take steps to mitigate them. If you're afraid of flying, you can educate yourself on the statistics. Or, you can speak to a professional about your fear to help you understand and manage it.

After all, you can't control what happens once you're in a situation, so there's no use in living your life in fear of something that's out of your control. Instead, focus on what you can control, such as your response to the emotion or your lack of knowledge about the activity you are participating in.

Some Fears Are Based on Circumstances

Our fears manifest themselves in different ways. Some of our fears are based on real-life circumstances that are out of our control. For example, if you're afraid of flying, it's because there's a chance that the airplane could crash. For me, I am a hypochondriac. One night I was home, enjoying a movie. When I touched the side of my head, I felt a bump, and a hot rash spread across my body. I panicked and scurried to the mirror to see the culprit: A mole. My mind spiraled with all the terrible and rare diseases it could be. I was convinced that I had skin cancer and would die a slow and painful death.

At that moment, I had to stop myself. I switched my thinking and thought about the best-case scenario: It's just a mole. The worst case: A cancerous mole. Then I broke the situation into steps. If the worst-case scenario were to happen to me, how concerned should I be? What are the next steps? What can I do about it? So, instead of going down a rabbit hole, I made an appointment with a dermatologist the same night for the next day's morning. It was inconvenient because I had plans for the following day, but my peace of mind is more important than anything else—I needed to face my fears.

So, I went to the doctor. The mole ended up being a regular mole, but the relief I felt was immeasurable. If I had let my fear control me, I would have continued to worry myself sick. If you can confirm that the worst-case scenario of your fear is not happening, do that as soon as you can. Your peace of mind is priceless.

Say Farewell to Your Fears

When I moved to the United States, I went to a theme park with my friends. They dragged me to hop on a rollercoaster. It wasn't a big ride, but I was terrified. I thought I would die. The little kids who rode them without hesitation amused me, though. Tired of my fear, I decided to explore it. I rode one of the tallest rollercoasters in the country. Then, I took a doors-off helicopter tour above Manhattan. After that, I went to Vegas and jumped off the Strat Hotel and rode all the rides on the roof as well.

My farewell to fear was skydiving in Hawaii. Yes, I jumped off a fucking plane. A person who couldn't ride a small rollercoaster without being dramatic jumped out of a plane 15,000 feet above the ground. Before jumping—to ease part of my fear—I read all the statistics about skydiving. I read about safety measures, the technologies behind them, and the probability of dying from skydiving. Knowledge is powerful against fear. When you understand what you're afraid of, the fear dissipates. When you have the data, you sound more credible to your brain when you explain that it's safe.

I remember the waiting period at that small airport—how hectic it was. My brain was cool with me jumping since I fed all the data to it and learned it was safe. However, my emotions and my body gave zero fucks about the data. I was shaking. When we started boarding the tiny plane, I felt my gut twist. I was terrified.

When the plane took off, I took a deep breath and told myself, *You're going to be fine.* I kept repeating it in my head. When it was my turn to jump, I said it one more time, firmly and reassuringly, "YOU GONNA BE FINE!" and jumped. I survived, and jumping out of the plane was one of the most exhilarating experiences of my life. Fears are just figments of our imagination. They are created by us and only have as much power as we give them.

I'm not just afraid of heights—I fear lots of shit, including but not limited to speeding, heights, natural disasters, animals, flying, and the list goes on. However, I decided to live and enjoy this life for myself. I will not hide under my bed my whole life. Fears won't keep me from having fun. I understand where my fears are coming from, I understand that it's a normal body response to different stress, and I acknowledge that most likely, I'm going to be just fine. So, every time I'm scared, I remind myself of all those things, and I just say, "You gonna be fine."

Instead of Evening Prayers

1. Is there something you want to do, but your

fear prevents you? What exactly are you afraid of and why?

2. Can you write down the best-case and very worst-case scenarios for this situation?

3. Do some research on how likely that worst-case scenario would take place and also what would happen should it occur.

4. What steps can you take to maximize the probability for the best-case scenario and compare it? Are you missing out simply because of fear?

17

— • —

DINERO

I like money. Do you like money? I think we can all agree that money is pretty fucking exceptional. It's a universal language, a motivator, and it makes the world go 'round. Here's the issue, though—money is also a very delicate subject. Many people are uncomfortable talking about money, and even more people are uncomfortable admitting that they don't know everything there is to know about money.

Money Is Not Bad

Let's get one fact straight: Money is not bad. In fact, money is neutral. Some people think money makes people greedy—that's not true. What people do with money is good or bad. Just like most everything in life, money is a tool that can be used for good or for bad. You shouldn't be afraid of money or think it's dirty or evil. Money is energy—a resource that can create, destroy, help, or harm. The key is to be mindful of your relationship with money. Money is a tool, and like any tool, it can be used wisely or foolishly.

Money can't make you happy, but it can solve a lot of problems. If I'm already unhappy, I'd rather work on bringing that happiness in a penthouse in Manhattan or in a gorgeous house overlooking the Spitting Cave in Oahu. How could money make your journey toward happiness a little easier?

You Are Not a Bank

A big mistake people make is thinking they are a bank and lending money to their friends or family. Money in your pockets doesn't make you a bank. A bank is a business that makes money by lending money to people who need it. They have risk management, assets and liabilities, a charter, and insurance coverage. You are not a bank, and you don't have this protection. You are not an investment firm. Don't think you're in the business of lending money. Lend money only to people you truly want to help, and only give what you can afford to lose. Then go in with the mindset that you will never get that money back, and be okay with it.

Save, Save, and Save Even More

Living paycheck to paycheck is not living—it's surviving, and just barely at that. If you want to get ahead, you need to save money. Now, after living in New York City, I understand it's not always easy, but if that's your case, you need to adjust your lifestyle. Don't do yourself dirty like that. Living below your means is not a crime. In fact, it will help you do more in the long run. Invest in yourself and your future by saving as much money as you can.

You become vulnerable when you live paycheck to paycheck because any tiny obstacle can send you into a tailspin. However, if you have savings, you have a cushion to fall back on. You have a safety net. That will give you peace of mind and the freedom to take risks.

It doesn't matter how much money you make; what matters is how much money you keep. Many people think an abundance of money leads to financial success, but that's not true. It's not how much money you make; it's how you manage your money and how much you're left with.

Honestly, to me, people who have zero dollars in their savings are like extraterrestrial beings. I'm sorry, but it's true. Of course, there are extraordinarily unfortunate and fucked-up situations, but in a general sense, if you have zero dollars in savings, you are not doing something right. Start saving now even if it's just $5, $10, or $20 a week.

I simply don't want to understand people who don't have a safety net. Savings are like a parachute. You don't need it until you really need it, but when you do—boy, oh boy, aren't you glad you have it. Many options are available to you to save money. You can use coupons, promos, research better deals, or other sales. However, I have one simple rule. Aim to save more than the cost of your time that you are investing.

Live According to Your Financials

Listen, having money in the bank doesn't mean we are spiraling out of control. Balling out is being reckless and is a sure way to end up flat-out broke. We don't stop living when we can't afford something. Needs and wants are different. You need food, water, and shelter. You want the newest iPhone, designer clothes, and to go on fancy vacations.

Be honest with yourself about what you can and can-not afford. Be smart about your purchases, and don't buy something solely because you can afford it. You can be too rich for your own good. Ask yourself if the purchase is going to improve the quality of your life or just give you a momentary high. If it's the latter, save your money and find another way to get that fix. Nothing is wrong with being frugal. In fact, I think it's a virtue.

If you want to make a purchase that is over 15% of your monthly income, think long and hard about it. I'm not saying don't do it, but really think about it. Weigh the pros and cons and decide if it's worth it. If it costs over 50% of your monthly income, consider buying something cheaper. A cheaper version with similar qualities and features is usually available. Look for coupons or promo codes. Do you know how easy they are to find? Just Google the store or website title and "promo codes." We Google everything else, so we can Google codes that save us thousands of dollars a year.

You can break your budgeting into groups using the 50/30/20 strategy. As a rule of thumb, 50% of your income goes toward needs, 30% toward wants, and 20% toward savings or debt repayment (NerdWallet, 2022). Of course, you should work toward improving these budgets. However, it can help you figure out where your money is going and how to manage it better.

Don't Be Afraid of Credit Cards

I know many people are afraid of credit cards because they've heard horror stories about people getting into debt and never being able to pay it off. While that is possible, you don't have to let it happen. Sure, credit cards can be scary, but if used responsibly, they are a great way to build your credit score, which is important for receiving a lower interest rate on loans, mortgages, and auto financing. A good credit score can save you a ton of money in the long run.

Many credit cards also offer benefits such as points, cash back, miles, special offers, and more. Plus, with a credit card, you're using the bank's money, which means if it gets stolen, they're more likely to offer solutions and protection. If used responsibly, a credit card can be a great tool to help you save money.

Of course, there are downsides to credit cards. If you're not careful, you can easily get into debt, which is why educating yourself on credit cards is necessary. Only spend what you can afford to pay back in full, and always make your payments on time. Treat it as your cash value. Be smart about using credit cards. If you have never used credit cards, educate yourself first. Talk to someone who's a pro at it. Read financial blogs. Use them smartly and benefit from them.

Invest

Investing should be a routine part of your financial life, just like saving and spending. Investing is how you achieve long-term financial goals, such as buying a house or retiring comfortably. You have a variety of investment options. You can invest in real estate, stocks, bonds, NFTs, crypto, and more.

You can pick what suits you and your budget but start now. The sooner you start, the more time your money has to grow. The more time your money has to grow, the more you will have later.

Take a percentage that you can afford from every paycheck and set up a recurring transfer. Make investing part of your routine. Diversify your portfolio, meaning don't put all your eggs in one basket. Choose different investments to protect yourself if one type loses value. Review your portfolio regularly and make changes as needed. As before, consult with experts and stay educated. Money doesn't respond well to impulsive or irrational treatment. Treat every dollar of yours with respect. Every dollar you earn should matter to you as a human being. Don't waste it.

Be Greedy—The Smart Way

Some people might say that being greedy is a bad thing. But with your finances, being greedy can actually be a good thing. Why? Being greedy means that you're always looking for ways to save money and grow your wealth. It means being proactive about your finances and always investigating how to improve your financial situation.

Greedy can mean smart spending, not overspending. It means looking for ways to save money, whether it's by couponing, negotiating bills, or cutting costs in other areas of your life. Don't be a reckless spender—be mindful of your habits.

You shouldn't be afraid to spend money on yourself. Remember what I said in Chapter 11? You are an investment, and you should absolutely spend the money you earn on yourself. Money is designed to be spent, anyway. However, being greedy means being mindful of how you spend your money. Make sure that you're getting the most bang for your buck. When it comes to your finances, being greedy means being smart, not wasteful. Don't spend more than you have. If you don't need a purchase, don't buy it. Don't fall into emotional spending, and always try to maximize the value of your buck.

Get a Side Hustle

The common problem: I don't have enough money to save or invest.

The solution: Get a side hustle.

A side hustle is a great way to make some extra money. In today's gig economy, more opportunities to start a side hustle exist than ever before, especially with internet use. You can use existing platforms to provide services like driving for Uber or Lyft or becoming an Airbnb host. You can start a blog, a podcast, and a YouTube channel and sell ads. You can create your own unique handmade products and sell them on Etsy. The options to make money are endless. The limits only exist within your ambitions and creativity.

You can get a new skill, switch careers, or look into passive income streams. Money doesn't fall from the sky—remember that. Once you start making extra money, you can start saving and investing. The key is to get started. Once you start, it becomes much easier to keep going.

Always Negotiate When It's Applicable

In today's world, we need to save money as often as possible, and one of the best ways to save money is to negotiate.

You can negotiate just about anything—your rent, salary, bills, and more. If you don't ask, you'll never get what you want. It doesn't matter if you're buying, selling, or renting—and I know this from experience. When I was living in New York City, my landlord would try to raise the rent every year, and I would negotiate.

To handle a successful negotiation, understand a couple of points:

- What value do you bring to the seller or customer?

- What value will they lose by losing you?

For example, when I was negotiating my apartment rent price, I thought about the value they would lose from me. First, they would have to renovate, which would cost labor and material. They would also lose out on income while the apartment was under construction, and they would have to look for another tenant, which could also take more time. Another concern was potentially having problematic tenants.

Then I considered my value. I paid on time and didn't cause any issues. The fifth-floor apartment was fine for me, even though there was no elevator. I took good care of my apartment and would renew it if they didn't change the price. Every time, it worked because the reward of keeping me outweighed the risk of losing me. Every situation is unique, so it's important to be mindful of the negotiation.

Analyze the situation thoroughly. Sometimes there could be a case when the market is so hot that the landlord wouldn't care. You would still want to negotiate, just on a softer side. Some people are afraid to negotiate because they think it'll make them look bad or pushy. However, if you don't negotiate, you'll always end up paying more or getting less than you should.

For example, another opportunity to negotiate would be for your compensation when you receive a job offer. It's important to know what your worth is. Don't sell yourself short just because you want the job or you think it'll make you look bad. Most companies have room for negotiation. Ask for what you deserve and continue negotiating until they back down. And remember, negotiation isn't just about getting more money—it can also mean getting more time, a better working environment, or other perks.

Instead of Evening Prayers

1. Do you have a savings account? If not, consider opening and contributing to it with every paycheck.

2. Do you have an investment portfolio? If not, get busy like it was yesterday. Learn and take steps toward having your own portfolio.

3. Do you pay for purchases with cash or debit cards? If yes, avoid it as much as possible. Educate yourself on credit cards and start using them.

4. Explore passive income streams and new skills you can develop to earn more money.

18

—◆—

FINDING YOUR WHALES

You know how every once in a while, you'll be going about your day, and you'll think to yourself, *What am I doing with my life?* We've all been there. You're not alone. The question of "What is the meaning of life?" has plagued philosophers and thinkers for centuries. What is the meaning of life for you? What do you think is the point? There is no single answer to this question.

Life Has No Purpose

It might sound morbid, but it's true: Life has no inherent purpose. We are not put on this earth for a specific reason. A grand plan, fate, or design doesn't exist. This can be a hard pill to swallow for some people. If you grew up in a religious household, you were probably taught that there is a specific reason for your existence. However, my truth is that life has no meaning, apart from the one we assign to it. This can be a liberating realization. It means that we have the power to create our own purpose.

You can always update your purpose, change it, and swap the priority order, but you must create it first. A life that matters to you is what you have to live. Create a legacy. It's your own responsibility. Some people rely on others to create the meaning and purpose of their lives. They might look to their parents, religion, or government to tell them what they should do, which is a recipe for disaster.

Relying on others to create your purpose is like giving someone else the keys to your life. You are handing over the power to control your life, and that is dangerous. To me, that's a really lazy tactic—wouldn't you be excited to explore the world and figure it out on your own? The quest for meaning is a lifelong journey, and it is one that you must embark on alone. No single answer will work for everyone. We all have to find our own way.

The Universe Is Yours

We are here for such a short time, and then we are gone. So, what is the point? What is the meaning of life? I believe that the meaning of life is what we make of it. We are the masters of our own destinies. We create our own meaning. However, that's a tough concept for some people to accept. They want someone else to tell them what to do and how to live their lives, but that is not living.

Nothing matters in the grand scheme of things, so we may as well assign our own meaning. When you realize nothing matters—the universe is yours—that is a beautiful thing. We have the power to create our own reality. The masters of our fates are ourselves. We can choose to live in a way that brings us joy and satisfaction.

The universe is yours for the taking. It is there for you to explore and discover. There are no rules; no one is telling you what to do. You can make your own rules. Whoever you want to be, you can be. You can do whatever you want. The world is your oyster. It is your playground. So, go out there and explore it. Find your own meaning and purpose. And let no one else tell you what you should or should not be doing with your life. Remember, no one gives a fuck about you, so you are the only one who can determine what is best for you. So, trust yourself and go out there and conquer the world.

No matter what you do or don't do in this life, you should always celebrate yourself. You are alive, and that is something to be grateful for. Every day is a new opportunity to create the life you want to live. So, celebrate every day. Life is limited and too precious to waste. It might sound cliché, but it's true. You only have one life to live, so make it count. Make it meaningful.

Life Is Based on Whales

For me, life is based around four whales: Knowledge, food, sex, and travel. These whales drive me, at least. I enjoy learning and growing, I'd die for a fantastic meal, I enjoy sex, and I couldn't imagine my life without traveling—I'm always on the go. Those whales bring me joy and meaning. I live with them. Currently, I think a new whale is being born for me because I'm getting more passionate about philanthropy. I don't know if it's going to grow enough to join my top four, but making the world better brings me joy. It's not big enough, but it's there. I see it, and I'm watching it closely, which is what you should be doing. You need to find your whales and watch them.

Find Your Whales and Go on a Journey

What I mentioned above are my whales, but they might not be yours. You might not need to travel or feel as passionate about food as I do. That's okay. We all have different passions that drive us. The journey to finding your whales is lifelong, but it's worth it. This journey is a quest for meaning and purpose. It will lead you to a life that is fulfilling and satisfying. Once you find your whales, hold on tight and enjoy the ride.

Go out with them and experience them to their fullest. Make mistakes. Take risks. Fail. Get back up and try again. Most importantly, enjoy the journey. Life is a beautiful gift, and it's even more gorgeous when you find your own meaning and purpose. So, go out there and find your whales. Never let go, and keep your spirit alive by moving forward.

However, remember, no matter how many whales you have, they are all in your head. You choose the whales. You are the only one who can create meaning in your life. So, don't wait for someone else to do it for you. Get out there and find your own way. Make your whales and journeys meaningful. It's just a big, fun game. At the end of the day, nothing really matters. We just have to do our best to enjoy this life as much as possible without losing our dignity. That's all that life is—a big game. So, have fun, be kind, be grateful, and enjoy the ride. Don't stop pursuing your quest. "What is the meaning of life?" is a question that has been asked throughout history, but it is one that we must each answer for ourselves.

Instead of Evening Prayers

1. What brings you universal joy?

2. What drives you to wake up in the morning?

19

— : —

MOTHER TERESA

Sometimes we want to help people, and other times we don't. We might be inclined to teach a newcomer at our job, but what about our annoying aunt who still can't figure out Facebook? Not so much. So, how do we know when to help and when not to? Occasionally, the pressure to help is so enormous that we can feel guilty when we don't. We might think that if we don't help, the person will fail or they won't like us. The truth is, we can't help everyone, and that's okay.

We can't always be there for people and shouldn't be expected to. We have to be mindful of our own limitations. Furthermore, we can't be available 24/7, and we can't be expected to know everything. It's important to set boundaries so that we don't get overwhelmed or taken advantage of. It's difficult to know when to say no, but it's important to do what's best for us.

The Two Conditions for Helping People

While we shouldn't expect something from the people we help, we do need one thing: Satisfaction. In order to be satisfied when helping someone, there are two conditions that must be met before we can offer our help. The first is that the person must want our help, and the second is that we must feel the need to help. If either of these two conditions is not met, it's best not to offer our help. Why? Well, you won't gain satisfaction from it.

The first condition, that the person must want our help, is important because if they don't want it, then they won't appreciate it. They won't value our help as much. It's like someone giving you a gift you don't really want. You might say *thank you*, but you won't be as grateful as if you had asked for it or picked it out yourself. The same goes for help. If the person didn't want it in the first place, they probably wouldn't value it as much. They might even be resentful, which can leave us feeling unsatisfied or bitter.

The second condition, that we must want to be of assistance, is important because if we don't want to help, then we won't be satisfied. We'll only be helping out of obligation, which also breeds resentment. We have to want to help out of the kindness of our hearts, or else the sentiment is useless.

It sounds harsh and maybe even selfish, but it's the truth. If you don't want to help and the other person doesn't want it, then you feel as though you have wasted your resources. You got nothing out of it, so you won't be happy. On the other hand, if you do want to help to feel as if you can be of help, then you will feel satisfaction because you will have helped in a way that was meaningful to both parties.

When you help someone, you should feel joy. Not everyone is going to need or want your help, and that's okay. You can't be everything to everyone. Know your limitations and only offer your help when you feel confident that you can be of assistance. This way, you'll be sure to get something out of it: Satisfaction.

In return, your help should be appreciated in terms of its application. This means if they use it, or it makes a difference in their lives. If you help somebody who never asked for it, they most likely will not appreciate it as much. They might not appreciate you and your efforts.

Here are some tips for you:

1. If you offer to help, be committed to it and put 100% effort into it.

2. Never exhaust your resources. You shouldn't suffer from helping others. Know your limits, and don't give more than you can.

3. Make sure the person is embracing or applying your help.

4. Be cautious of manipulations. If you helped someone once, make sure that person won't manipulate you and take advantage of your kindness by overusing you.

If You Don't Want to Help—Don't

As I mentioned above, if you won't receive satisfaction from helping someone, then don't. You don't have to help anybody if you don't want to. It's that simple. If someone needs help, that doesn't mean you're obligated to help them. You don't owe anyone shit. You can't help everyone, and you shouldn't feel guilty if you can't or don't want to be Mother Teresa. There's no shame in not wanting to help a person.

Help is like a coin. It has two sides: The helper and the helpee. Nothing is wrong with either side. Both have their own needs and are important, but you always must take care of yourself first. Keep in mind that you want to be satisfied, which means you both have to be on the same page. They have to want help, and you have to want to help.

However, sometimes saying no can be a struggle. Finding the balance between explaining yourself while still being polite and maintaining transparency can be difficult. You shouldn't feel like you owe anyone an explanation or reasoning for your action, but if you still want to have that transparency, here are a few tips on how to say *no* to the request:

1. Be firm. But not rude.

2. Don't explain why you are not able to help.

3. Thank them for the trust they displayed in seeking help from you.

4. If you can, offer them an alternative. Maybe share your experience and knowledge you have to get them started in the right direction.

If They Don't Ask, Don't Tell

Someone could use your help, but that doesn't mean they want it. It's important to respect the boundaries of others and not force our help on others. Sometimes the best way to help is just to be there for someone. Listen to them, and offer advice if they want it, but don't try to fix their problems for them.

There's a difference between venting and actually wanting help. When people vent, they want to get something off their chest. They don't actually want or need your help; they just want to talk. It's important to listen to people when they vent, but don't try to fix their problems for them. Just be there for them and let them share. If they want your help, they'll ask for it. The same goes for advice. Not everyone will want to hear the advice you may have. If they want your advice, they'll ask for it.

People are products of their decisions. If they're not happy with their lives, it's because of the decisions that they've made—decisions that we're not responsible for. Other people's problems are not our problems, and we can't help everyone, so don't feel bad for losers. Just focus on the people who matter and are trying to improve their lives.

Don't Feel Bad for Losers

While we should be empathetic toward others, there is a limit. We shouldn't feel bad for losers—people who are always bitching and moaning about their lives.

People who are always negative and have nothing good going on in their lives, and people who always find something to complain about. We shouldn't feel bad for them because they're not trying to make their lives better.

We can't always be there for people, and we can't always help them. Sometimes, people just need to deal with their own shit. I understand we don't all come into this world with the same benefit packages. I'm not talking about extreme cases; I'm talking about average people, like your sister or high school friend who has a shitty job and constantly complains without making changes. You can't feel bad for them because they're not trying to help themselves. If they live that life, it means they are okay with it, even if they say they aren't.

Also, You Aren't God

Sometimes we see a broken soul and feel the urge to save them. We may subconsciously think we are better than them or believe we're their saviors. But we are not gods, and we shouldn't play this game. We can't fix people. That's unnecessary, silly, and unethical. It's not your job to fix and save somebody. It's their journey, not yours. Let people deal with their own shit, especially if no one asks you for help.

Concentrate on yourself and don't play God.

Before trying to help someone else, ensure that your needs are met first. This might mean you have to focus on yourself for a bit and put your needs above others. You could have to say *no* to someone who needs your help. This doesn't make you a bad person; it just means that you must take care of your being first. It's normal and healthy to prioritize yourself.

Even if you want to help someone, however, your own needs should be satisfied. You need to ensure you're in a good place before trying to help someone else. To give fully, your basic needs should be established and satisfied.

Exceptions

An exception exists to every rule, and the same goes for asking for help. If you feel like doing something nice, you can help with a minor task without being asked. Generally, this applies to strangers. For instance, maybe you can help someone load groceries in their car, help an old lady across the street, give a stranger directions, or call an ambulance for a sick train passenger.

Those minor tasks are generous and usually appreciated. However, if you want to do something bigger for someone, make sure you know they want your help and that they will appreciate it. You don't want to be a nuisance. If you want to help and they don't want it, it'll only make the situation worse. Remember, both people need to be on the same page about receiving and giving help for the action to be satisfactory.

Instead of Evening Prayers

1. Have you ever helped someone but did not feel appreciated? Or maybe they didn't use the advice? Think back and try to remember if they asked for help or you offered.

2. Has there been a time when someone needed help, and you did it despite not wanting to? Was the experience satisfying?

3. Was there a time you helped someone and felt extremely happy afterward? Why do you think that was?

20

— ◆ —

Healthy Relationships (HR)

As humans, we are social creatures. Most of us thrive in relationships and connections with others, but what does it mean to have a healthy relationship? Far too often nowadays, we hear about toxic relationships and *reel* relationships, causing us to have misconceptions about maintaining a healthy relationship.

A healthy relationship is built on trust, mutual respect, and communication. It is a partnership where both people feel like they are equal contributors. Each person feels like they can openly express their thoughts, opinions, and feelings without fear of judgment or ridicule. In a healthy relationship, both people can compromise and negotiate disagreements. Lastly, a healthy relationship should make you feel good about yourself; it should not be draining or negative. If you find yourself in a relationship that is not meeting these standards, it may be time to reassess the situation.

From the moment you meet someone, you are already in a relationship with them. The way you interact and communicate with them will determine the quality of that relationship. Whether it's a positive or negative relationship is up to you.

There are four key components to a healthy relationship:

- **Trust**: Trust is the foundation of any relationship. In order for a relationship to be healthy, both parties need to trust one another. This means being honest and transparent with each other, being reliable and keeping your word, and respecting each other's privacy.

- **Respect**: This goes hand in hand with trust—both parties need to respect each other. This means that you should listen to each other, respect each other's thoughts and feelings, and think about each other's needs.

- **Communication**: This component is essential in any relationship. Both people should be comfortable communicating openly and honestly with each other. This means sharing your thoughts, feelings, and concerns with each other. It also includes listening to and understanding each other.

- **Compromise**: Not everyone is going to agree all the time. Both parties need to compromise with each other. This means been willing to meet in the middle to find a solution that works for both of you.

Don't Play Games

One common issue in relationships is playing games. This can take many forms, such as playing hard to get, leading someone on, or even gaslighting. Books, articles, magazines, and much more often provide tips on how to date and suggest being unavailable or unapproachable so we don't seem thirsty. Some tips may include "don't text right away," "don't show up on time," "act uninterested," and so on. What these tips don't take into consideration is that playing games is manipulative and can hurt the other person's feelings. Fuck that shit—save yourself the emotional turmoil.

Games are often used to control the other person and/or the relationship. They can be harmful and cause a lot of pain and hurt. Why would you even want to start your story with manipulations, anyway? Who in their right mind would want such a foundation for their relationship? If you like someone, act as you already do. Respond to their texts as quickly as you want to. Don't be afraid to show your emotions, and don't be scared to empathize with them. The worst outcome that can happen is that the person is not on the same page with you. In that case, you're not vibing, and it's time to move on.

However, if you're pretending to be someone you're not and/or playing games, you're only setting yourself up for disappointment and heartache. Even if that person does vibe with you, they're vibrating with the wrong version of you—the version you're pretending to be. So, be honest with yourself and the other person.

Don't lead them on or play with their feelings. Don't do anything you wouldn't want other people to do to you. If you're not interested, just say so. It's better to be honest upfront rather than string them along and give them false hope. If you are interested, then put your cards on the table and let the other person know. Don't play games or try to control the situation. Just go with your true emotional flow and see what happens.

The bottom line is that games are for kids. If you want a real, adult relationship, then act like it. Be yourself and be honest. It's the only way to build a solid foundation of trust and respect. Everything else is just a waste of time.

Emotional maturity is not always aligned with our physical maturity. Being in your 20s, 30s, 40s, or even 60s doesn't mean that your emotional self is on the same level. If you're still acting like a child, then chances are you're not ready for a mature relationship. It's time to grow up and start acting like the responsible adult you are. That means being honest, communicating effectively, and being yourself.

It also means setting boundaries and respecting the boundaries of others. If you can't do that, then you're not ready for a mature relationship. You must be emotionally developed and look for the same in a partner. Life is too short for unnecessary drama. Spend that time on love and joy instead. Find someone who is on the same page as you, and build a foundation of trust and respect.

"It's Complicated"

Facebook states that "it's complicated" is a relationship status. I'd like to disagree and say that "it's complicated" is a life status. Life might be complicated sometimes, but relationships have no right to be. Complicated relationships shouldn't exist. A relationship should be a refuge from the complications of life, not another source of them. A relationship should be your safe place. It should bring you a sense of joy, protection, and comfort. Keep the relationship simple.

The best relationships are the ones where both partners can be themselves without feeling like they have to put on a show or pretend to be someone they're not. Simplicity doesn't mean the relationship is perfect—no relationship is perfect. There will be arguments and disagreements. That's normal, but the key is to keep the situation simple and not make it more complicated than it needs to be.

Don't Be Afraid to Be Alone

There is nothing wrong with being single. In fact, there are a lot of benefits to being single. You have more time to focus on your career, your hobbies, and your personal growth. You don't have to compromise on your plans or put anyone else's needs above your own, and you don't have to answer to anyone but yourself. These qualities might seem selfish, but they're actually incredibly important for your mental and emotional health.

Of course, being in a relationship has its own set of benefits, but that doesn't mean that being single is a bad thing. Yet, society seems to suggest otherwise. We are constantly bombarded with messages that tell us we need to be in a relationship to be happy, successful or considered normal.

These messages are harmful, and they can make single people feel like there is something wrong with them. They can make us feel like we need to find a partner as soon as possible, even if we're not really ready for a relationship, or stay in terrible relationships because we're afraid of being alone. As a result, some people constantly surround themselves with others to avoid being alone, even if they're not thrilled with their relationships. They get into a relationship with anybody just to avoid being alone.

What are you scared of? Are you scared of yourself? Maybe it's time to get to know yourself better. It could be really beneficial for some to do a relationship detox or even a social detox. When you are in peace, when it's quiet—you can hear your true self. Go on a date with yourself sometimes. Take yourself on a solo trip—get to know you. You should never depend on someone. You should always be able to count on yourself first.

I'm a true believer that we should learn to be totally comfortable being on our own before starting any serious relationship. Being able to enjoy solitude, do activities alone, and be comfortable with yourself is a superpower. We need to understand who we are and what we want first. How can we know who would be a suitable partner for us if we don't know ourselves?

Avoid People Who Are Insecure

In relationships, it's important to be with someone who feels secure in themselves. It's not just about being physically secure, but also emotionally and mentally secure. This applies to any relationship—friends, family, partners; however, it's especially important in romantic relationships. Many people are insecure, and they don't even realize it. They might be insecure about their looks, their intelligence, or their abilities. While it's okay to have some insecurities, it's not okay to let them take over your life or your relationship.

People who are insecure tend to be jealous, controlling, and possessive. They might try to isolate you from your friends and family. They might try to control what you wear or how you act, or constantly try to one-up you or make you feel inferior. Insecure people are exhausting to be around. They are always seeking validation and attention, which can be really draining. If you're in a relationship with someone who is insecure, these qualities will affect you and maybe even rub off on you. You're exposed to these negative qualities more often and on a more intimate level, so it's important to be aware of them.

Insecure people will eventually get comfortable with you. They'll feel safe, which will turn into bravery. They might start picking on you and testing you out. Insecure people often feel their whole life—their whole world—is unfair. Since they can't express themselves, stick up for themselves, or set boundaries in the outside world, they will take it out on you—the person who is closest to them. They crave that winner's rush.

After they've experienced unfortunate events, some of these people picture themselves defeating the bad guy in their thoughts in the shower. They rehearse saying this or that instead of being silent. They like the idea of who they can be, so they take their rehearsals to the stages of life. You become their little playground.

Instead of defeating the bad guys in real life, they are dramatic and fight over minor issues with you. To outsiders, they may seem like the "good" one in your relationship, and if you say otherwise, people find it hard to believe. If you run into someone like that, it's a red flag. Stay alert and, better yet, stay away. It's not your job to "fix" them or "save" them.

Secure people are different. They don't need validation from others to feel good about themselves. They're confident, and they trust themselves. They know their worth and don't need to put others down to feel better about themselves. And they don't need to control or possess the people in their lives. Secure people are comfortable with themselves, and they're comfortable with you. They don't feel the need to constantly check in on you or keep tabs on you. They don't feel threatened by your success or your happiness. And they don't feel the need to one-up you or make you feel inferior.

If you're in a relationship with a secure person, you'll feel safe. You'll feel like you can be yourself without being judged. You'll feel like you can express yourself without being shut down and be successful without anyone feeling threatened. However, you also need to acknowledge if you're the insecure person in the relationship.

It's important to work on yourself and your own insecurities so that you can be a secure, confident person. If you're not secure, you'll never be able to truly be yourself—and that's not fair to you or your partner. A variety of tools can help you identify the causes of your insecurities and work through them.

Creating and Maintaining a Healthy Relationship Isn't Difficult

Many people think that having a healthy, long-lasting relationship is hard work. But it doesn't have to be. Yes, it takes effort to make a relationship work, but it shouldn't be difficult. To create a healthy relationship, you need to be with someone who respects you, loves you, and makes you feel good about yourself. If you're with someone who does none of that, then it's time to move on.

To maintain a healthy relationship, you need to communicate with your partner. Talk about what you're feeling, what you want, and what you're thinking. Don't bottle yourself up, and be empathetic. How would you feel if you were in their shoes? It's also important to be supportive of your partner. Be there for them when they need you. Lastly, trust is essential in any relationship. If you can't trust your partner, then the relationship will not work.

50/50 Looks Different in Every Relationship

There's talk about what 50/50 should be in a relationship. I recently watched a TikTok video of a woman saying 50/50 should always be you pay half the bill and do half the housework, and the same goes for your partner. Another woman chimed in and said that's not 50/50 because if one person is working more hours than the other, then they're doing over 50%. The comments were filled with people arguing over what 50/50 actually should be.

Personally, I think 50/50 looks different in every relationship because every relationship is different. You can't put a one-size-fits-all label on it. If your friend's relationship works a certain way, that doesn't mean yours will too. The key is to find what works for you and your partner.

One partner might be better at problem-solving, while the other might be better at handling responsibilities. Maybe one partner stays home while the other goes to work. One might be better at communicating, while the other is better at listening. We all have unique skill sets and personal qualifications. Just as you would apply for a job that fits within your limitations, the same goes for a relationship. You need to have your skills complement each other.

In some cases, this might mean one person takes on the major burden of certain tasks because that's where their strength lies. For example, if one person is better at handling finances, they might take care of the bills. If one person is better at cooking, then they might do most of the meal prep. That doesn't mean the other person isn't helping—they just might help in other ways.

On the same hand, if you need help in your areas, then delegate where your partner can use their strengths. If you're doing taxes, maybe they're great at organizing, so they can help you get everything together. If you're planning a trip, maybe they're great at finding good deals, so they can help you save money. They can help you see the situation more clearly if you are feeling overwhelmed.

Communicate with each other about what you both need and want. Not one person should have 100% of the work on their shoulders all the time. Their workloads can be different; they can be relative. You don't want to get burned out, but neither should your partner. If you are the person who may rely on their partner heavily, acknowledge them. Thank them. Appreciate them. Help in your own way as much as possible. Small gestures can make a big difference.

The goal is to find a balance that works for both of you without either person feeling like they're being taken advantage of. It might take some trial and error, but it'll be worth it in the end to have a supportive and fulfilling partnership.

You Are Not the "Other Half"

We all have nicknames for our partners. For some couples, these nicknames are cutesy and affectionate, like "baby," "my love," or "honey." They might start out that way, but too often, they become a way of diminishing our partners and ourselves. We call them our "better halves" or our "other halves." As if we are incomplete without them. As if they somehow "complete" us.

Of course, this relates to the old legend of the God who split human beings in two because we were too perfect. So, he separated us and set us wandering the Earth looking for our missing halves. The search is supposed to end when we find the person who makes us feel "whole." To be honest, this story has always bothered me. It suggests that we are less than whole human beings without romantic partners. It perpetuates the false idea that we are not complete without someone else.

Not that partnerships and marriage aren't important. To me, they are, but to think that your partner is your other half is demeaning. This way of thinking about relationships is not only damaging; it's wrong. It suggests that we are incomplete without our partners, and that we cannot be whole without them. It puts an unhealthy amount of pressure on the relationship and on our partners to "fix" us and make us happy and complete. However, do you ever think about yourself as something that is incomplete?

Call your significant other a soulmate, lover, or whatever else, but please don't call them your other half and especially not the "better half." We are all whole human beings, whether we are in a relationship or not. All of us are complete on our own. We don't need another person to make us whole. Of course, relationships can enhance our lives and make us happier, but they cannot "complete" us. Only we can do that.

Honestly, when people equate themselves with their partner as a whole, it is an enormous problem. Some people lose their identity and keep saying "we" when talking about anything. They mimic their partner's habits and preferences. It's totally normal to a certain extent, but you can't just erase your personality. Staying true to who you are is what you have to do. You are not a single organism. You are the union of two individuals.

If you think about it, it's really sad when you put your partner on a pedestal and expect them to make you happy. No one can make you happy except for yourself. Find happiness within yourself first, before you can truly be happy in a relationship. If you're not happy with yourself, how can you expect someone else to make you happy?

You and your loved one should grow on your own but side by side. Work on being the best version of yourself, and don't put pressure on your partner to "complete" you.

So, please, for the sake of yourself and your relationship, don't think of your partner as your other half. Think of them as your equal, best friend, or partner in crime, but they are not responsible for making you whole. You are responsible for that. When you realize that, you will not only be happier, but you will also be a better partner.

Love and the Devil Hide in the Details

Some people might say that love is blind, but I think it's more accurate to say that love hides in the details. It's the little things that you do for each other that add up to create a strong and lasting bond. It's not about grand gestures or big romance—it's about the day-to-day actions that show you care.

For example, maybe you know your partner likes their coffee in a certain way. So, you make it just the way they like it some mornings without them even having to ask. Or perhaps you know they're going through a tough time at work, so you surprise them with their favorite dinner to show them you're thinking of them.

It's the little things that show you're paying attention and that you care. They might not seem like much, but they make a big difference in a relationship. These details add up over time to create a strong and lasting bond. Pay attention to your partner. Listen to details and do little cute acts of kindness from time to time. It'll make a world of difference. It really is the little things that matter.

My friend Justin's wife, Susie, recently shared their love story with me. On their first date, they went to a lovely coffee shop and chatted for a bit. At some point, their conversation turned to books, and Susie briefly mentioned that her favorite childhood book was *The Little Prince* by Saint-Exupéry.

She forgot that she had told him about this minor fact until her birthday a few months later. Justin invited her to a restaurant and gave her a gift. What she unwrapped was a copy of *The Little Prince*, but the version had been published the year she was born.

It was adorable and touching to Susie—she couldn't hold back her tears! Justin paid attention to a minor detail and turned it into a charmingly lovely moment.

Communicate

Communication is a vital part of any relationship, but it's especially important if you're in one. We tend to forget this, but people aren't mind-readers. Your partner might know you well, but they can't read your mind. If you want your partner to better understand you or make a specific change, you need to communicate with them. Talk to them about your needs and explain how their behavior is affecting you. Be open, honest, and direct. Vulnerability is okay—that's how you build intimacy and trust in a relationship.

Tell them who you are and why you're hurt, rather than attacking them. Take responsibility for your own feelings and communicate them in a way that is respectful and constructive. If you're feeling insecure, try to share those feelings with your partner instead of lashing out at them.

Also, ensure you're being respectful when communicating with your partner. Listen to what they say. Don't interrupt them or talk over them. Try to see the situation from their perspective. This can be difficult, but they're their own person with their own thoughts and feelings. When you share, be sure to use "I" statements. For example, say, "I feel _____ when you _____." This will help your partner understand how you're feeling without assigning them blame. Respect your partner's boundaries and listen to them if they need space or time to process what you've said.

Don't Humiliate Your Partner

I'm sure we've all seen it before: The partner who constantly puts their partner down in front of others. Maybe they do it in a "joking" way, but it's really just a way to control and humiliate their partner. Or maybe you've witnessed a couple who argue in the street or gloat about their partner's worst qualities and how "stupid" they are. This is not a healthy relationship.

This is not only disrespectful but also a form of emotional abuse. People do this to control and undermine their partners. If you're constantly putting them down, they're going to believe it. They'll doubt themselves and their worth. That's not fair to them or to the relationship. You love them because of certain qualities, not despite them. So, why would you want to make them feel bad about themselves?

A healthy relationship is built on mutual respect, trust, and communication. If you're constantly putting your partner down, you're not respecting them. You're not valuing their thoughts or feelings, and you're certainly not listening to them or trying to understand their perspective.

A partner who loves and respects you will never publicly humiliate you. They might tease you or make jokes, but it will always be good fun. They won't try to put you down or make you feel inferior, and they definitely won't try to control you. If your partner is constantly putting you down, it's time to have a serious talk with them about your relationship. If they can't see how hurtful their actions are, then maybe this isn't the right relationship for you. Remember, though, that it's a two-way street. If you're constantly putting your partner down, that's not healthy either.

Support Your Partner Deeply

Relationships also require emotional support, which is one of the greatest aspects of having a partner because you have your own personal support system. In a healthy relationship, your partner will be there for you when you need them. This support goes beyond just being there for each other when you're happy or sad. It's about being emotionally present for each other, even when you don't quite understand what they're going through.

A suitable partner will be your shoulder to cry on, your sounding board, and your biggest cheerleader. Through thick and thin, they will support you. They'll be there for you when you're feeling down or struggling with something. They'll listen to you, offer advice if you want it, and just be there for you. It's okay to lean on them and rely on them. In fact, that's what they're there for.

Your partner should also support your dreams and goals. They should root for you every step of the way. Even if you don't believe in yourself, they should believe in you. They should be there to encourage you and help you achieve your dreams. As with the other qualities, though, support is a give and take. You shouldn't expect your partner to support you if you don't support them in return. Build your partner up in the way you want to be built up. If they want to start a new hobby, career, or project, be their biggest fan. If they need your help to achieve something, offer it without hesitation.

Give Your Partner Space

Your partner might be "yours," but that doesn't mean they belong to you. Your partner doesn't literally have to be your ball and chain. Being in a relationship doesn't mean you have to be attached at the hip. Taking time apart and doing your own thing is healthy. This can be anything from taking a solo trip, going out with friends, or just spending some time alone.

They're their own person with their own thoughts, feelings, and dreams. Give your partner the space they need to be themselves. It's okay for you to be an introvert and for them to be an extrovert. As a couple, you can each have different interests. You don't always have to do the same things together—especially if you don't want to. However, that also means you don't have to force them to accompany you because you're not comfortable going alone.

Your interests make you unique and distinct. What's important is respecting each other's differences and giving each other the space to be yourselves. Giving your partner space is especially important if they are going through tough times. They might need some time alone to sort themselves out, which is okay. Of course, we love and care for them, which makes us want to be there for them, but sometimes the best we can do is give them some space. We have to remember that we are all different. We handle our problems differently, we cope differently, and we need different kinds of support. You might want someone with you if you were going through a tough situation, but that doesn't mean your partner feels the same way.

You Don't Own Your Partner

As I stated above, you don't own your partner. They are their own person with their own thoughts, feelings, and desires. It's important to respect their autonomy.

You are partners. You are best friends. Both of you are beautiful but separate individuals. You are a team. None of you should be an accessory to the other. You don't want to be only recalled and identified as someone's spouse, girlfriend, boyfriend, partner, etc. You want to be portrayed as a stand-alone person, the person who is complete without the other. Your title as a partner should come after [insert who you are].

Respect Your Partner's Privacy

Privacy can be a funny issue in relationships. We want to know everything about our partners, but we also want them to respect our privacy. The balance is tricky to find, but having some privacy in a relationship is important. This doesn't mean you have to keep secrets from each other, but there are some things that are just for you.

Part of being in a relationship is sharing your life with another person, but that doesn't mean you have to share every single detail. You can still have hobbies, friends, and interests that are just for you. It's okay to have some secrets that your partner doesn't know about. It can actually make you more interested in them. They'll be curious about what you're up to, which can add excitement to the relationship.

Of course, there is such a thing as too much privacy. If you're keeping secrets from your partner that are important, that's not healthy. If you're not being honest about your feelings or what you're doing, that can lead to problems in the relationship. However, if you're just keeping a few secrets to yourself, that's perfectly normal and healthy.

Many people struggle with privacy because they think it means they're not fully committed to the relationship. Maybe you're someone who has given too much privacy to the wrong person in the past, and it led to them cheating or lying to you. Understandably, you would fear that happening again, but you must try to trust your partner because your current relationship has nothing to do with your former experience. If you can't trust, then why be in a relationship?

Humans Are Emotional—Understand That

We are all human, and we have emotions. Relationships don't erase our emotions. In fact, being in a relationship can sometimes amplify our emotions. Sometimes, our emotions have nothing to do with our partner, and yet because we are so close to them, they can get caught in the crossfire.

Understanding that we are emotional creatures and that sometimes we just need to feel our emotions, even if they don't make sense, can be a big and crucial step in having a healthy relationship. You or your partner might be annoyed, angry, or irritated sometimes, especially after a long day at work or when dealing with other stressors in life, and that's okay. It's normal to feel like that.

Sometimes we unintentionally let the dog off the leash, and our emotions come out as yelling or worse. It's okay to be emotional, and it's also okay that we cannot control ourselves all the time. If this happens, do not escalate the situation and take some time to calm down because taking it out on your partner is not okay. We shouldn't want to hurt them, so it's best to take a breather. Mistakes happen, and sometimes we forget our manners and act like children. As a result, we should "punish" ourselves like children. Separate yourself from the situation. Think about what you've done and why. What are you angry about? What's going on? Once you've calmed down, you can talk to your partner about it and apologize.

Step away from each other, cool down and talk about what happened after. Let your partner know you acknowledge their emotions. Maybe you can remind them you love each other and suggest a timeout.

You can revisit when you both feel more at ease and can sift through the feelings constructively instead of lashing out.

Love Is Not Pain

Love doesn't have to hurt. Many people think that love is supposed to be this all-consuming, passionate feeling that's also painful, but that's not necessarily true. Love can be passionate, but it doesn't have to hurt. A healthy relationship is built on trust, respect, and communication. It's not built on drama or pain.

If your relationship hurts you more than it makes you happy, then it's not a healthy relationship—something is wrong. Don't stay in a relationship because you're afraid of being alone. That's not a good enough reason. Find someone who makes you happy—someone who treats you well. You deserve to be happy. Don't settle for anything less.

Drama Is Not Romantic

Drama might make for good television, but it doesn't make for a good relationship. Many people view relationships as nothing more than a series of highs and lows, but this is actually incredibly unhealthy. Stability in a relationship is a necessity. You want to count on the other person. When you have drama, it's because one or both of you are not behaving in a healthy way, and it will only damage your relationship.

Drama is often created by people who are insecure or have control issues. They need constant reassurance that they're still wanted or needed and will go to great lengths to get it. This often manifests as jealousy, when someone becomes possessive and paranoid about their partner. They might constantly check their phone, accuse them of cheating, or try to control who they talk to and what they do. This is not healthy, and it's not how a relationship is supposed to be.

Some people also romanticize drama, thinking that it's what makes a relationship passionate. They believe that fighting and making up will keep the spark alive and that make-up sex is the best sex. This might be true in the movies, but it's not true in real life. In reality, all that drama is exhausting and not worth it.

While it's normal to have disagreements, they should be healthy disagreements that are resolved constructively. Drama is not romantic; it's toxic garbage. We don't collect garbage, remember? We collect joy. If love doesn't bring you joy, then you have garbage and a major problem on your hands.

Passion is amazing, but remember that passion is not the same as drama. Passion is intense and exciting, but it's not destructive. It doesn't involve tearing each other down; it's about building each other up. A relationship should be a safe space, a place where you can be yourself and where you know the other person has your best interests at heart. It should be a source of strength and support, not a source of drama and stress. So, if you find yourself in a relationship that's nothing but drama, it might be time to hit the eject button.

Ultimatums Should Have a Follow Through

No one likes ultimatums. Ultimatums are pretty much someone's way of saying, "You're going to fucking do it my way, or your life will become Hell," and sometimes we really struggle with compromising—especially if it goes against a hardcore belief.

In general, I'm not a fan of ultimatums, but I can understand their efficacy in extreme cases. However, the problem often arises when one provides an ultimatum but doesn't follow through. This is an empty threat, and it will only serve to further anger and upset your partner. I'm not saying you give your partner ultimatums, but what I am saying is that if you're going to resort to threats or manipulation, you better be prepared to follow through.

For example, threaten to break up or get a divorce only if you're actually planning on following through. Some couples, during any brief fight, will threaten to leave each other. Most often, they don't, or if they do, they return the next day, receiving the "on again, off again" title. This is unhealthy, and it confuses your partner.

It also makes ultimatums seem like nothing more than another way to control them because that's what they are: A manipulation tactic. They threatened to leave because they wanted something from their partner, and when their partner didn't give in—they left. The goal was to control the other person by making them feel useless on their own.

It's not a healthy way to communicate, and it will only serve to further damage your relationship. However, as I said, sometimes ultimatums might be necessary. Maybe you and your partner have been together for 10 years, and you want to get married, but they're not ready. You've talked about it for the last three years, and they still don't want to take that next step. In this case, you could give them an ultimatum: Either we get married in six months, or I'm leaving.

This is a pretty big ultimatum, but if you feel as if you're at your wit's end and marriage is something you really want, then you need to be prepared to follow through.

You may also want to explain to them why. Maybe to you, since the relationship won't progress further, then it's already reached its peak and is over. Either way, you're attempting to convey how important the situation is to you.

Of course, there's always the possibility that your partner will call your bluff, and you'll have to leave. In this case, you need to be prepared for the consequences. It might hurt them, and maybe even yourself, but ultimatums are worthless if you don't have genuine intentions and don't follow through. Respect yourself, respect your partner, and respect each other's time. If something is bothering you, talk to each other first before resorting to extreme tactics.

Instead of Evening Prayers

1. What comes to mind when you think about your partner? Can you list the qualities you love about them? During the next week, pick one of those qualities and tell your partner how much you appreciate them. Give examples of

them executing this quality. Thank them. You will realize how impactful this appreciation can be. Make it a regular habit.

2. Is there something you dislike or is bothersome about your partner's behavior? If yes, select a day and create a space to talk about it when both of you are available.

3. Do you support your partner in pursuing their goals? Talk to them and ask how you can help. It's important to empower them constantly and provide genuine support.

4. Do you ever manipulate your partner? Answer this honestly. Would you want your partner to treat you the way you treat them?

5. Are you independent from your partner mentally, financially, and socially? If no, why not?

21

THE OUTSIDERS

The world is a massive place filled with many people. Most of them, you don't know; most of them, you don't care about. They're just background noise—the faceless masses. You might interact with them on a day-to-day basis, like with the cashier at the grocery store or the person who sits next to you on the bus. However, even then, you don't really know them, and you shouldn't care about them. You should feel absolutely NUMB to the outsiders.

Yet, we feel the need to put labels on them, to group them together and make assumptions about them, or to impress them with our own labels and groupings, but at the end of the day, we're all just individuals. We're all just people. That's all we really are, which is why it's important to pay attention to what you put into the outside world and how you treat others.

Social Media

We spoke about social media in an earlier chapter; however, I think it's worth talking about one more time. In this day and age, social media is a big part of our lives. It's how we stay connected with our friends and family. We get our news from social media, and that's how we stay up-to-date on the latest trends. It's also how we project our image to the world.

Privacy should be taken seriously with social media. You never know who is watching or who might see what you're posting. Develop a privacy hygiene routine. You shouldn't keep your full legal name, phone number, address, date of birth, or any other sensitive information online. Of course, there may be exceptions, such as if you run a business, especially one online. However, the goal here is to not have your information easily accessible to anyone who might want to find it. People shouldn't be able to look you up online easily. You want to be as private to the outsiders as possible.

Also, when it comes to social media, you should be careful about what you post—that is not the space to publish your deepest, darkest secrets. That's what this book is for. Social media should project a positive image of yourself to the world. It should be a highlight reel of your life. Of course, you don't have to put on a fake persona and only show the good parts of your life, but you also don't need to overshare.

Pick what you want to share with the world, and be mindful of how you want to be perceived. Some people might say that social media is "fake" because we only show the good parts of our lives, but that's okay. That's how it is. We're all just trying to put our best foot forward. Most of your followers probably give zero fucks about your wisdom, tips, or anything else you share.

In my opinion, the best strategy for building a social media image is to keep personal business to yourself and keep it fun, funny, and humble. You don't have to be an attention whore unless you are an influencer. I find it hot when some people appear too cool and busy for social platforms. They show up occasionally, but the rest of the time they are mysterious stallions.

Don't Overthink

Yeah, the world is filled with millions of people—but should you care about what they all think? No. You should only care about what the people who matter think—the people who you love and who love you—your family and friends, and the people who are in your inner circle. That's it. Everyone else is just background noise. So, don't overthink the situation. Don't try to please everyone. If you tried to please everyone, you would end up pleasing no one—including yourself. It's better to be yourself and to only care about the people who matter.

Additionally, don't read into what other people say or do. Sometimes people might use a certain tone with us or give us a look, and we interpret it in our own way. We might overthink and overanalyze. This can be especially true when it comes to text messages. However, we shouldn't care so much. Even if we're interpreting the messages the right way, the way we handle our lives is none of their business. We cannot control them, so we should move on.

Also, don't compare yourself to others. Do your own thing. Facebook, Instagram, and other social media platforms can make it easy to compare ourselves to others. We see their highlight reels, and we think that's what their lives are really like. But that's not always the case. There's a difference between "reel" and "real." People only post the good parts of their lives online. The only person you can compare yourself to is yourself—the "you" from yesterday, a month ago, a year ago, or a decade ago. That's the only person you should compete with—yourself.

The perfect pictures and the staged moments might make you envious, but that's not reality. Their lives aren't truly like that. You might never know what their genuine life is like, but you do know what your life is like. So, focus on that. Focus on your own life and your own journey. If someone's life looks perfect, that doesn't mean it's true. So, don't compare yourself to others. You never know what somebody is going through behind closed doors. Just focus on your own life and be grateful for what you have.

Stop Arguing With People

As I said, there are people everywhere. Everyone has their own opinion, experiences, and beliefs. It's rare that you'll find someone who thinks and acts 100% like you. Honestly, imagine if we did. Imagine if we were all the same—the world would be boring as fuck.

However, as I said, we get so offended when someone questions our thoughts and beliefs. We feel the need to argue our point and stick up for ourselves. While there's nothing wrong with defending your beliefs, there's no need to argue with people. If you're debating with someone, and they're not trying to understand your point of view, then they're not worth your time.

Arguing with people is a waste of time and energy. It's pointless because you're never going to change a stubborn mind. And even if you do, what does it matter? They're still entitled to their own opinion. I would say don't argue ever, but I don't think that's possible for humans, so at least don't argue with strangers. With family and friends, an argument could be a fun debate, or maybe because of your relationship, they might see the situation from your point of view. But with strangers, it's not worth it. Especially online.

Make it a golden rule: No arguing.

Avoid Social Traps

We're adults, right? We know what's good for us and what's not. We should be able to make our own decisions, yet we often let others influence us. We are not children anymore; we don't have to listen to what others tell us. We don't have to follow a path that society has created for us. Fuck the outsiders and their expectations.

However, sometimes we do it anyway. Social traps can be subtler than following the crowd. It can be peer pressure or the feeling that you need to keep up with others. It can be FOMO or imposter syndrome. Whatever form it takes, social traps are incredibly harmful.

They prevent us from living our best life and being true to ourselves. We need to learn to recognize these traps and avoid them.

- Don't want kids? Great, don't have them.

- Don't want to go to college? That's perfectly fine too.

- Don't want to get married? You do you, boo.

- Don't like pets? Don't pretend as if you do.

The world is your oyster. Do what makes you happy. Life is too short to live someone else's blueprint.

Don't Waste Time on Stupid Shit

No one is going to do your work for you. Take the initiative and make your goals happen. If you want something, go out and get it. Don't sit around waiting for someone else to make it happen.

Don't waste time on things that don't matter. If something is stressing you out, then do what you can to rid yourself of the worries. Redirect your attention to what makes you happy. Life is too short to waste on bullshit.

Bottom line: Don't sweat the small stuff, and don't be afraid to go after what you want.

If you want to be successful, you need to focus on what's important. You need to focus on your goals and what you need to do to achieve them. You can't afford to waste time on things that don't matter, such as outsiders' opinions or actions.

I'm not saying you need to work 24/7, but you need to be productive with your time. Use your time wisely, and don't let distractions get in the way. For example, I struggled with this when I was writing this book. This book has been on the back burner of my mind for the last two years. I spoke about it with my friends and gloated about how I was going to write this amazing book that would change people's lives, but then I didn't do anything about it right away.

I was comparing myself to others and afraid that my writing skills were not sophisticated enough. I was concerned about what people would think of me and was too focused on the outsiders instead of just creating what my heart desired.

No one is going to do the work for you. Be willing to put in the time and effort to make your dreams a reality. So, stop wasting your time on stupid shit. Stop talking about it, get off your ass, and actually do what you want. Don't put time and energy into people who show you they don't want it. Do whatever the fuck you want with your life. Just don't be wasteful.

Time is your currency to get into life's experiences. Don't waste it on outsiders. Don't worry about what they think, how they perceive you, or how they might judge you. These people are not important. You probably won't even see them more than once. The main character in your life is you. It is your life.

Don't Show Off

Most of us do like to show off, especially if someone has mistreated us in the past. We may want to prove to them that we are better than them, that we are more successful, and have a more joyful life. This little competition in life is normal, but something we need to work on. We need to remove the competitive quality from our personalities.

We shouldn't care about impressing others. It's a waste of time and stupid. Before showing off, answer these questions:

- What am I trying to achieve by showing off?

- What will I gain?

- Do these people even matter?

- Is it my ego that I'm trying to please?

So, instead of trying to show off, focus on being genuine and authentic. Please don't compare your life to someone else's, and don't try to make others think that you have it all perfect. Just mind your own business and be happy with what you have.

This doesn't mean that you can't strive for more. This doesn't mean that you can't have goals and work hard to achieve them. But don't do it for the wrong reasons. Don't do it to show off. Do it because you want to better yourself and your life. You should do it because it makes you happy, not because you want to impress outsiders. You shouldn't feel the need to impress anyone. If you do, it's time to have an honest talk with yourself because the only person you should try to impress is you. It's always you versus you. Work toward being better than you were yesterday— keep impressing the past version of yourself. You are the only one who will follow you until the ends of the Earth.

Instead of Evening Prayers

1. How do you think the outside world portrays you? Do you like that image? Do you care? Should you care?

2. Are there any social traps you have fallen into? If yes, can you eliminate at least 50% of them? Put just a bit more effort into not giving a fuck about traps.

CONCLUSION

Congratulations! You have completed NUMB. Take a moment to reflect on your experience. Are there points you agree with? Did you learn anything that surprised you? Did this book challenge your views of yourself or the world in any way? Can you think of any points I made that you disagreed with?

At its core, NUMB is a book about self-empowerment and the importance of living life to the fullest. It challenges conventional notions of success and happiness and encourages you to pursue your dreams, despite whatever obstacles you may face along the way. As I said before, I don't want you to agree with everything I said in this book—I want you to question and challenge your beliefs about yourself, the world, and everything in between.

This book is largely based on my life and my circumstances, but I believe that the lessons it contains are universal. I hope that NUMB can help you find your way back to yourself and begin living a life on your own terms. So, go forth, embrace the chaos of life, and never be afraid to think for yourself. For it is only by embracing the uncertainty that we can truly live our best lives, and isn't that what NUMB is all about?

If you enjoyed reading NUMB, I highly encourage you to leave a review and share your thoughts with others. Thanks for reading, and I wish you all the best on your journey ahead!

About Author

Pasha Tay is, as you would call it, a street-smart philosopher. He is a first-generation American who fled from an eastern European country with no social support, money, or English language skills. His diverse life experience taught him how to fight back, own his mistakes, and turn failures into successes. Today, he is a writer, interpreter, songwriter, engineer, and investor who craves to give back by sharing his discoveries about life with the readers like you.

@NUMB.BOOK

@PASHA.TAY

REFERENCES

Allen, D. (n.d.). *1-on-1: David Allen's two minute rule time-management tips from the expert.* https://www.bishophouse.com/wp-content/upload s/2018/01/1-on-1-David-Allens-Two-Minute-Rule.p df

Foley, L. (2020, March 17). *When should you replace your mattress?* Sleep Foundation. https://www.sleepfoundation.org/mattress-in formation/when-should-you-replace-your-mattress

Jacobson, B. H., Boolani, A., & Smith, D. B. (2009). Changes in back pain, sleep quality, and perceived stress after introduction of new bedding systems. *Journal of Chiropractic Medicine,* 8(1), 1–8. https://d oi.org/10.1016/j.jcm.2008.09.002

NerdWallet. (2022, January 28). 50/30/20 *Budget cal-culator.* NerdWallet. https://www.nerdwallet.com/a rticle/finance/nerdwallet-budget-calculator

WCNC Staff. (2019). *Stressed? Worrying is a waste of your time, experts say.* Wcnc.com. https://www.wcnc.com/article/news/local/wake-up-charlotte/stressed-worrying-is-a-waste-of-your-time-experts-say/275-517236ed-b890-4cba-b671-827911a87f9f

Young, J. (2020, May 5). *Researcher behind "10,000-hour rule" says good teaching matters, not just practice.* EdSurge. https://www.edsurge.com/news/2020-05-05-researcher-behind-10-000-hour-rule-says-good-teaching-matters-not-just-practice

Made in the USA
Las Vegas, NV
13 January 2024

84310440R00174